MznLnx

Missing Links Exam Preps

Exam Prep for

Beginning and Intermediate Algebra The Language And Symbolism Of Mathematics

Hall, Mercer, 1st Edition

The MznLnx Exam Prep is your link from the texbook and lecture to your exams.
The MznLnx Exam Preps are unauthorized and comprehensive reviews of your textbooks.

All material provided by MznLnx and Rico Publications (c) 2010
Textbook publishers and textbook authors do not particpate in or contribute to these reviews.

MznLnx

Rico Publications

Exam Prep for Beginning and Intermediate Algebra The Language And Symbolism Of Mathematics
1st Edition
Hall, Mercer

Publisher: Raymond Houge
Assistant Editor: Michael Rouger
Text and Cover Designer: Lisa Buckner
Marketing Manager: Sara Swagger
Project Manager, Editorial Production: Jerry Emerson
Art Director: Vernon Lowerui

Product Manager: Dave Mason
Editorial Assitant: Rachel Guzmanji
Pedagogy: Debra Long
Cover Image: Jim Reed/Getty Images
Text and Cover Printer: City Printing, Inc.
Compositor: Media Mix, Inc.

(c) 2010 Rico Publications

ALL RIGHTS RESERVED. No part of this work covered by the copyright may be reproduced or used in any form or by an means--graphic, electronic, or mechanical, including photocopying, recording, taping, Web distribution, information storage, and retrieval systems, or in any other manner--without the written permission of the publisher.

For more information about our products, contact us at:

Dave.Mason@RicoPublications.com

For permission to use material from this text or

product, submit a request online to:

Dave.Mason@RicoPublications.com

Printed in the United States
ISBN:

Contents

CHAPTER 1
Operations with Real Numbers — 1

CHAPTER 2
Linear Equations and Patterns — 19

CHAPTER 3
Lines and Systems of Linear Equations in Two Variables — 33

CHAPTER 4
Linear Inequalities and Systems of Linear Inequalities — 47

CHAPTER 5
Exponents and Operations with Polynomials — 56

CHAPTER 6
Using Common Algebraic Functions — 72

CHAPTER 7
Another Look at Factoring Polynomials — 86

CHAPTER 8
Radical Expressions, Complex Numbers, and Quadratic Equations — 94

CHAPTER 9
Rational Expressions — 113

CHAPTER 10
Exponential and Logarithmic Functions — 127

CHAPTER 11
A Preview of College Algebra — 134

ANSWER KEY — 141

TO THE STUDENT

COMPREHENSIVE

The *MznLnx* Exam Prep series is designed to help you pass your exams. Editors at MznLnx review your textbooks and then prepare these practice exams to help you master the textbook material. Unlike study guides, workbooks, and practice tests provided by the texbook publisher and textbook authors, *MznLnx* gives you **all** of the material in each chapter in exam form, not just samples, so you can be sure to nail your exam.

MECHANICAL

The MznLnx Exam Prep series creates exams that will help you learn the subject matter as well as test you on your understanding. Each question is designed to help you master the concept. Just working through the exams, you gain an understanding of the subject--its a simple mechanical process that produces success.

INTEGRATED STUDY GUIDE AND REVIEW

MznLnx is not just a set of exams designed to test you, its also a comprehensive review of the subject content. Each exam question is also a review of the concept, making sure that you will get the answer correct without having to go to other sources of material. You learn as you go! Its the easiest way to pass an exam.

HUMOR

Studying can be tedious and dry. MznLnx's instructional design includes moderate humor within the exam questions on occassion, to break the tedium and revitalize the brain

Chapter 1. Operations with Real Numbers

1. _____ or arithmetics is the oldest and most elementary branch of mathematics, used by almost everyone, for tasks ranging from simple daily counting to advanced science and business calculations.
   a. Thing
   b. Arithmetic0
   c. Undefined
   d. Undefined

2. _____ is a branch of mathematics concerning the study of structure, relation and quantity.
   a. Algebra0
   b. Concept
   c. Undefined
   d. Undefined

3. An _____ is a combination of numbers, operators, grouping symbols and/or free variables and bound variables arranged in a meaningful way which can be evaluated..
   a. Expression0
   b. Thing
   c. Undefined
   d. Undefined

4. The mathematical concept of a _____ expresses the intuitive idea of deterministic dependence between two quantities, one of which is viewed as primary and the other as secondary. A _____ then is a way to associate a unique output for each input of a specified type, for example, a real number or an element of a given set.
   a. Function0
   b. Thing
   c. Undefined
   d. Undefined

5. _____ are the basic objects of study in graph theory. Informally speaking, a graph is a set of objects called points, nodes, or vertices connected by links called lines or edges.
   a. Graphs0
   b. Thing
   c. Undefined
   d. Undefined

6. _____ is a synonym for information.
   a. Data0
   b. Thing
   c. Undefined
   d. Undefined

7. A _____ is a one-dimensional picture in which the integers are shown as specially-marked points evenly spaced on a line.
   a. Number line0
   b. Thing
   c. Undefined
   d. Undefined

8. In mathematics, a _____ may be described informally as a number that can be given by an infinite decimal representation.
   a. Real number0
   b. Thing
   c. Undefined
   d. Undefined

9. In statistics, a _____ is a graphical display of tabulated frequencies.
   a. Histogram0
   b. Concept
   c. Undefined
   d. Undefined

10. The _____ (symbol _____) and the millibar (symbol mbar, also mb) are units of pressure.
    a. Bar0
    b. Thing
    c. Undefined
    d. Undefined

Chapter 1. Operations with Real Numbers

11. In mathematics, a _____ is a two-dimensional manifold or surface that is perfectly flat.
    a. Plane0
    b. Thing
    c. Undefined
    d. Undefined

12. _____ means of or relating to the French philosopher and mathematician René Descartes.
    a. Thing
    b. Cartesian0
    c. Undefined
    d. Undefined

13. _____ element of an element x with respect to a binary operation * with identity element e is an element y such that x * y = y * x = e. In particular,
    a. Thing
    b. Inverse0
    c. Undefined
    d. Undefined

14. In mathematics, the _____ inverse, or opposite, of a number n is the number that, when added to n, yields zero. The _____ inverse of n is denoted −n.
    a. Additive0
    b. Thing
    c. Undefined
    d. Undefined

15. In mathematics, the _____ of a number n is the number that, when added to n, yields zero. The _____ of n is denoted −n. For example, 7 is −7, because 7 + (−7) = 0, and the _____ of −0.3 is 0.3, because −0.3 + 0.3 = 0.
    a. Thing
    b. Additive inverse0
    c. Undefined
    d. Undefined

16. In mathematics, a _____ can mean either an element of the set {1, 2, 3, ...} (i.e the positive integers or the counting numbers) or an element of the set {0, 1, 2, 3, ...} (i.e. the non-negative integers).
    a. Natural number0
    b. Thing
    c. Undefined
    d. Undefined

17. In mathematics, a _____ number is a number which can be expressed as a ratio of two integers. Non-integer _____ numbers (commonly called fractions) are usually written as the vulgar fraction a / b, where b is not zero.
    a. Rational0
    b. Thing
    c. Undefined
    d. Undefined

18. In mathematics, a _____ can mean either an element of the set {1, 2, 3, ...} (i.e the positive integers) or an element of the set {0, 1, 2, 3, ...} (i.e. the non-negative integers).
    a. Whole number0
    b. Concept
    c. Undefined
    d. Undefined

19. The _____ are the only integral domain whose positive elements are well-ordered, and in which order is preserved by addition. Like the natural numbers, the _____ form a countably infinite set. The set of all _____ is usually denoted in mathematics by a boldface Z .
    a. Integers0
    b. Thing
    c. Undefined
    d. Undefined

20. In mathematics, an _____ number is any real number that is not a rational number- that is, it is a number which cannot be expressed as a fraction m/n, where m and n are integers.

Chapter 1. Operations with Real Numbers

a. Irrational0
b. Thing
c. Undefined
d. Undefined

21. In mathematics, an _____ is any real number that is not a rational number ¡ª that is, it is a number which cannot be expressed as m/n, where m and n are integers.
    a. Thing
    b. Irrational number0
    c. Undefined
    d. Undefined

22. In mathematics, _____ are any real number that is not a rational number ¡ª that is, it is a number which cannot be expressed as m/n, where m and n are integers.
    a. Thing
    b. Irrational numbers0
    c. Undefined
    d. Undefined

23. In mathematics and the mathematical sciences, a _____ is a fixed, but possibly unspecified, value. This is in contrast to a variable, which is not fixed.
    a. Constant0
    b. Thing
    c. Undefined
    d. Undefined

24. A _____ is a symbolic representation denoting a quantity or expression. It often represents an "unknown" quantity that has the potential to change.
    a. Variable0
    b. Thing
    c. Undefined
    d. Undefined

25. _____ is the state of being greater than any finite real or natural number, however large.
    a. Infinite0
    b. Thing
    c. Undefined
    d. Undefined

26. A _____ is a number that is less than zero.
    a. Thing
    b. Negative number0
    c. Undefined
    d. Undefined

27. In mathematics, the _____ of a coordinate system is the point where the axes of the system intersect.
    a. Thing
    b. Origin0
    c. Undefined
    d. Undefined

28. _____ is a mathematical notation for describing a set by stating the properties that its members must satisfy.
    a. Set-builder notation0
    b. Thing
    c. Undefined
    d. Undefined

29. Mathematical _____ is used to represent ideas.
    a. Thing
    b. Notation0
    c. Undefined
    d. Undefined

30. In mathematics, the additive inverse, or _____ of a number n is the number that, when added to n, yields zero. The additive inverse of n is denoted −n. For example, 7 is −7, because 7 + (−7) = 0, and the additive inverse of −0.3 is 0.3, because −0.3 + 0.3 = 0.

a. Opposite0
b. Thing
c. Undefined
d. Undefined

31. The _____ of measurement are a globally standardized and modernized form of the metric system.
    a. Units0
    b. Thing
    c. Undefined
    d. Undefined

32. A _____ is the result of the addition of a set of numbers. The numbers may be natural numbers, complex numbers, matrices, or still more complicated objects. An infinite _____ is a subtle procedure known as a series.
    a. Thing
    b. Sum0
    c. Undefined
    d. Undefined

33. Mathematical _____ are the wide variety of ways to capture an abstract mathematical concept or relationship.
    a. Representations0
    b. Thing
    c. Undefined
    d. Undefined

34. An _____ is an equality that remains true regardless of the values of any variables that appear within it, to distinguish it from an equality which is true under more particular conditions.
    a. Thing
    b. Identity0
    c. Undefined
    d. Undefined

35. In mathematics the _____ of a set which is equipped with the operation of addition is an element which, when added to any other element x in the set, yields x.
    a. Concept
    b. Additive identity0
    c. Undefined
    d. Undefined

36. The _____ of a mathematical object is its size: a property by which it can be larger or smaller than other objects of the same kind; in technical terms, an ordering of the class of objects to which it belongs.
    a. Magnitude0
    b. Thing
    c. Undefined
    d. Undefined

37. In mathematics, the _____ (or modulus) of a real number is its numerical value without regard to its sign.
    a. Absolute value0
    b. Thing
    c. Undefined
    d. Undefined

38. The _____ integers are all the integers from zero on upwards.
    a. Nonnegative0
    b. Thing
    c. Undefined
    d. Undefined

39. _____ are objects, characters, or other concrete representations of ideas, concepts, or other abstractions.
    a. Thing
    b. Symbols0
    c. Undefined
    d. Undefined

40. In mathematics, an inequality is a statement about the relative size or order of two objects. For example 14 > 10, or 14 is _____ 10.

Chapter 1. Operations with Real Numbers

a. Thing
b. Greater than0
c. Undefined
d. Undefined

41. In mathematics, an _____ is a statement about the relative size or order of two objects.
    a. Inequality0
    b. Thing
    c. Undefined
    d. Undefined

42. In common philosophical language, a proposition or _____, is the content of an assertion, that is, it is true-or-false and defined by the meaning of a particular piece of language.
    a. Statement0
    b. Concept
    c. Undefined
    d. Undefined

43. Equivalence is the condition of being _____ or essentially equal.
    a. Thing
    b. Equivalent0
    c. Undefined
    d. Undefined

44. _____ is the state of being greater than any finite number, however large.
    a. Infinity0
    b. Thing
    c. Undefined
    d. Undefined

45. _____, either of the curved-bracket punctuation marks that together make a set of _____
    a. Parentheses0
    b. Thing
    c. Undefined
    d. Undefined

46. In elementary algebra, an _____ is a set that contains every real number between two indicated numbers and may contain the two numbers themselves.
    a. Interval0
    b. Thing
    c. Undefined
    d. Undefined

47. In geometry, an _____ is a point at which a line segment or ray terminates.
    a. Endpoint0
    b. Thing
    c. Undefined
    d. Undefined

48. A _____ of a number is the product of that number with any integer.
    a. Thing
    b. Multiple0
    c. Undefined
    d. Undefined

49. _____ is the notation in which permitted values for a variable are expressed as ranging over a certain interval; "5 < x < 9" is an example of the application of _____.
    a. Interval notation0
    b. Thing
    c. Undefined
    d. Undefined

50. In plane geometry, a _____ is a polygon with four equal sides, four right angles, and parallel opposite sides. In algebra, the _____ of a number is that number multiplied by itself.

a. Square0
b. Thing
c. Undefined
d. Undefined

51. In mathematics, a _____ of a number x is a number r such that r^2 = x, or in words, a number r whose square (the result of multiplying the number by itself) is x.
   a. Thing
   b. Square root0
   c. Undefined
   d. Undefined

52. In mathematics, a _____ of a complex-valued function f is a member x of the domain of f such that f(x) vanishes at x, that is, x : f (x) = 0.
   a. Thing
   b. Root0
   c. Undefined
   d. Undefined

53. _____ is the calculated approximation of a result which is usable even if input data may be incomplete, uncertain, or noisy.
   a. Concept
   b. Estimation0
   c. Undefined
   d. Undefined

54. In geographic information systems, a _____ comprises an entity with a geographic location, typically determined by points, arcs, or polygons. Carriageways and cadastres exemplify _____ data.
   a. Thing
   b. Feature0
   c. Undefined
   d. Undefined

55. In arithmetic and algebra, when a number or expression is both preceded and followed by a binary operation, an _____ is required for which operation should be applied first.
   a. Thing
   b. Order of operations0
   c. Undefined
   d. Undefined

56. A _____ is a quantity that denotes the proportional amount or magnitude of one quantity relative to another.
   a. Ratio0
   b. Thing
   c. Undefined
   d. Undefined

57. A _____ decimal is a decimal fraction which ends after a definite number of digits.
   a. Terminating0
   b. Thing
   c. Undefined
   d. Undefined

58. _____ is a way of expressing a number as a fraction of 100 per cent meaning "per hundred".
   a. Percent0
   b. Thing
   c. Undefined
   d. Undefined

59. The term _____ can refer to an integer which is the square of some other integer, or an algebraic expression that can be factored as the square of some other expression.
   a. Thing
   b. Perfect square0
   c. Undefined
   d. Undefined

Chapter 1. Operations with Real Numbers 7

60. A _____ decimal is a number whose decimal representation eventually becomes periodic (i.e. the same number sequence _____ indefinitely).
   a. Thing
   b. Repeating0
   c. Undefined
   d. Undefined

61. The act of _____ is the calculated approximation of a result which is usable even if input data may be incomplete, uncertain, or noisy.
   a. Estimating0
   b. Thing
   c. Undefined
   d. Undefined

62. _____ the expected value of a random variable displays the average or central value of the variable. It is a summary value of the distribution of the variable.
   a. Thing
   b. Determining0
   c. Undefined
   d. Undefined

63. An _____ or member of a set is an object that when collected together make up the set.
   a. Thing
   b. Element0
   c. Undefined
   d. Undefined

64. In mathematics, the _____ , or members of a set or more generally a class are all those objects which when collected together make up the set or class.
   a. Thing
   b. Elements0
   c. Undefined
   d. Undefined

65. A bar chart, also known as a _____ , is a chart with rectangular bars of lengths usually proportional to the magnitudes or frequencies of what they represent.
   a. Thing
   b. Bar graph0
   c. Undefined
   d. Undefined

66. In mathematics, there are several meanings of _____ depending on the subject.
   a. Degree0
   b. Thing
   c. Undefined
   d. Undefined

67. _____ is the study of terms and their use — of words and compound words that are used in specific contexts.
   a. Thing
   b. Terminology0
   c. Undefined
   d. Undefined

68. An _____ is a number which is involved in addition. Numbers being added are considered to be the addends.
   a. Addend0
   b. Thing
   c. Undefined
   d. Undefined

69. A _____ is a numeral used to indicate a count. The most common use of the word today is to name the part of a fraction that tells the number or count of equal parts.
   a. Thing
   b. Numerator0
   c. Undefined
   d. Undefined

Chapter 1. Operations with Real Numbers

70. A _____ is the part of a fraction that tells how many equal parts make up a whole, and which is used in the name of the fraction: "halves", "thirds", "fourths" or "quarters", "fifths" and so on.
    a. Denominator0
    b. Concept
    c. Undefined
    d. Undefined

71. _____ is a concept in traditional logic referring to a "type of immediate inference in which from a given proposition another proposition is inferred which has as its subject the predicate of the original proposition and as its predicate the subject of the original proposition (the quality of the proposition being retained)."
    a. Concept
    b. Conversion0
    c. Undefined
    d. Undefined

72. A _____ is a negotiable instrument instructing a financial institution to pay a specific amount of a specific currency from a specific demand account held in the maker/depositor's name with that institution. Both the maker and payee may be natural persons or legal entities.
    a. Thing
    b. Check0
    c. Undefined
    d. Undefined

73. In abstract algebra, _____ consists of sets with binary operations that satisfy certain axioms.
    a. Thing
    b. Grouping0
    c. Undefined
    d. Undefined

74. In financial mathematics, the _____ volatility of an option contract is the volatility _____ by the market price of the option based on an option pricing model.
    a. Thing
    b. Implied0
    c. Undefined
    d. Undefined

75. In mathematics, _____ is an elementary arithmetic operation. When one of the numbers is a whole number, _____ is the repeated sum of the other number.
    a. Thing
    b. Multiplication0
    c. Undefined
    d. Undefined

76. _____, from Latin meaning "to make progress", is defined in two different ways. Pure economic _____ is the increase in wealth that an investor has from making an investment, taking into consideration all costs associated with that investment including the opportunity cost of capital.
    a. Thing
    b. Profit0
    c. Undefined
    d. Undefined

77. The _____, the average in everyday English, which is also called the arithmetic _____ (and is distinguished from the geometric _____ or harmonic _____). The average is also called the sample _____. The expected value of a random variable, which is also called the population _____.
    a. Thing
    b. Mean0
    c. Undefined
    d. Undefined

78. Regrouping is the act of putting ones into groups of 10. For example, the 1 on the far right of 131 would be denoted _____ if the digit of the number being subtracted is larger than 1, such as 131-99.

a. By 100
b. Thing
c. Undefined
d. Undefined

79. _____ is the distance around a given two-dimensional object. As a general rule, the _____ of a polygon can always be calculated by adding all the length of the sides together. So, the formula for triangles is P = a + b + c, where a, b and c stand for each side of it. For quadrilaterals the equation is P = a + b + c + d. For equilateral polygons, P = na, where n is the number of sides and a is the side length.
   a. Perimeter0
   b. Thing
   c. Undefined
   d. Undefined

80. In topology and related areas of mathematics a _____ or Moore-Smith sequence is a generalization of a sequence, intended to unify the various notions of limit and generalize them to arbitrary topological spaces.
   a. Thing
   b. Net0
   c. Undefined
   d. Undefined

81. In business, particularly accounting, a _____ is the time intervals that the accounts, statement, payments, or other calculations cover.
   a. Period0
   b. Thing
   c. Undefined
   d. Undefined

82. _____ is a temperature scale named after the German physicist Daniel Gabriel _____ , who proposed it in 1724.
   a. Thing
   b. Fahrenheit0
   c. Undefined
   d. Undefined

83. _____ is a physical property of a system that underlies the common notions of hot and cold; something that is hotter has the greater _____ .
   a. Temperature0
   b. Thing
   c. Undefined
   d. Undefined

84. _____ is the property of a physical object that quantifies the amount of matter and energy it is equivalent to.
   a. Mass0
   b. Thing
   c. Undefined
   d. Undefined

85. In geometry, a _____ (Greek words diairo = divide and metro = measure) of a circle is any straight line segment that passes through the centre and whose endpoints are on the circular boundary, or, in more modern usage, the length of such a line segment. When using the word in the more modern sense, one speaks of the _____ rather than a _____ , because all diameters of a circle have the same length. This length is twice the radius. The _____ of a circle is also the longest chord that the circle has.
   a. Thing
   b. Diameter0
   c. Undefined
   d. Undefined

86. In mathematics a _____ is a function which defines a distance between elements of a set.
   a. Metric0
   b. Thing
   c. Undefined
   d. Undefined

87. The _____ is a decimalized system of measurement based on the metre and the gram.
   a. Metric system0
   b. Concept
   c. Undefined
   d. Undefined

88. A _____ is the sum of the elements of a sequence.
   a. Series0
   b. Thing
   c. Undefined
   d. Undefined

89. A _____ is a special kind of ratio, indicating a relationship between two measurements with different units, such as miles to gallons or cents to pounds.
   a. Thing
   b. Rate0
   c. Undefined
   d. Undefined

90. A _____ is a unit of length, usually used to measure distance, in a number of different systems, including Imperial units, United States customary units and Norwegian/Swedish mil. Its size can vary from system to system, but in each is between 1 and 10 kilometers. In contemporary English contexts _____ refers to either:
   a. Thing
   b. Mile0
   c. Undefined
   d. Undefined

91. _____ is a unit of speed, expressing the number of international miles covered per hour.
   a. Miles per hour0
   b. Thing
   c. Undefined
   d. Undefined

92. A _____ or CD is a time deposit, a financial product commonly offered to consumers by banks, thrift institutions, and credit unions.
   a. Thing
   b. Certificate of deposit0
   c. Undefined
   d. Undefined

93. _____ finance, in finance, a debt security, issued by Issuer
   a. Thing
   b. Bond0
   c. Undefined
   d. Undefined

94. _____ is a kind of property which exists as magnitude or multitude. It is among the basic classes of things along with quality, substance, change, and relation.
   a. Amount0
   b. Thing
   c. Undefined
   d. Undefined

95. _____ is often used to describe the measurement of the steepness, incline, gradient, or grade of a straight line. The _____ is defined as the ratio of the "rise" divided by the "run" between two points on a line, or in other words, the ratio of the altitude change to the horizontal distance between any two points on the line.
   a. Slope0
   b. Thing
   c. Undefined
   d. Undefined

96. In geometry, an _____ of a triangle is a straight line through a vertex and perpendicular to (i.e. forming a right angle with) the opposite side or an extension of the opposite side.

a. Altitude0
b. Concept
c. Undefined
d. Undefined

97. _____ is a payment made by a company to its shareholders
   a. Thing
   b. Dividend0
   c. Undefined
   d. Undefined

98. The _____ of a ring R is defined to be the smallest positive integer n such that $n\,a = 0$, for all a in R.
   a. Characteristic0
   b. Thing
   c. Undefined
   d. Undefined

99. In mathematics, a _____ is an ordered list of objects. Like a set, it contains members, also called elements or terms, and the number of terms is called the length of the _____. Unlike a set, order matters, and the exact same elements can appear multiple times at different positions in the _____.
   a. Sequence0
   b. Thing
   c. Undefined
   d. Undefined

100. In probability theory, _____ are various sets of outcomes (a subset of the sample space) to which a probability is assigned.
   a. Events0
   b. Thing
   c. Undefined
   d. Undefined

101. A _____ is a number, figure, or indicator that appears below the normal line of type, typically used in a formula, mathematical expression, or description of a chemical compound.
   a. Thing
   b. Subscript0
   c. Undefined
   d. Undefined

102. _____ in 1557.
   a. Robert Recorde0
   b. Person
   c. Undefined
   d. Undefined

103. A _____ is a set of possible values that a variable can take on in order to satisfy a given set of conditions, which may include equations and inequalities.
   a. Thing
   b. Solution set0
   c. Undefined
   d. Undefined

104. The plus and _____ signs are mathematical symbols used to represent the notions of positive and negative as well as the operations of addition and subtraction.
   a. Thing
   b. Minus0
   c. Undefined
   d. Undefined

105. In geometry, a _____ is defined as a quadrilateral where all four of its angles are right angles.
   a. Rectangle0
   b. Thing
   c. Undefined
   d. Undefined

106. A _____ is a system of payment named after the small plastic card issued to users of the system.

Chapter 1. Operations with Real Numbers

    a. Thing
    b. Credit card0
    c. Undefined
    d. Undefined

107. In banking and accountancy, the outstanding _____ is the amount of money owned, or due, that remains in a deposit account or a loan account at a given date, after all past remittances, payments and withdrawal have been accounted for.
    a. Thing
    b. Balance0
    c. Undefined
    d. Undefined

108. In mathematics, a _____ or rhodonea curve is a sinusoid plotted in polar coordinates.
    a. Thing
    b. Rose0
    c. Undefined
    d. Undefined

109. _____ or investing is a term with several closely-related meanings in business management, finance and economics, related to saving or deferring consumption.
    a. Investment0
    b. Thing
    c. Undefined
    d. Undefined

110. In mathematics, a _____ is the result of multiplying, or an expression that identifies factors to be multiplied.
    a. Thing
    b. Product0
    c. Undefined
    d. Undefined

111. In mathematics, factorization (British English: factorisation) or factoring is the decomposition of an object (for example, a number, a polynomial, or a matrix) into a product of other objects, or _____, which when multiplied together give the original.
    a. Thing
    b. Factors0
    c. Undefined
    d. Undefined

112. In mathematics, _____ is a property that a binary operation can have. Within an expression containing two or more of the same associative operators in a row, the order of operations does not matter as long as the sequence of the operands is not changed.
    a. Thing
    b. Associativity0
    c. Undefined
    d. Undefined

113. In mathematics, the _____ inverse of a number x, denoted 1/x or x^{-1}, is the number which, when multiplied by x, yields 1. The _____ inverse of x is also called the reciprocal of x.
    a. Multiplicative0
    b. Thing
    c. Undefined
    d. Undefined

114. The _____ of a solid object is the three-dimensional concept of how much space it occupies, often quantified numerically.
    a. Thing
    b. Volume0
    c. Undefined
    d. Undefined

Chapter 1. Operations with Real Numbers 13

115. In classical geometry, a _____ of a circle or sphere is any line segment from its center to its boundary. By extension, the _____ of a circle or sphere is the length of any such segment. The _____ is half the diameter. In science and engineering the term _____ of curvature is commonly used as a synonym for _____.
   a. Thing
   b. Radius0
   c. Undefined
   d. Undefined

116. _____ is the fee paid on borrowed money.
   a. Interest0
   b. Thing
   c. Undefined
   d. Undefined

117. An _____ is the fee paid on borrow money.
   a. Concept
   b. Interest rate0
   c. Undefined
   d. Undefined

118. In mathematics, a _____ is an n-tuple with n being 3.
   a. Thing
   b. Triple0
   c. Undefined
   d. Undefined

119. Initial objects are also called _____, and terminal objects are also called final.
   a. Thing
   b. Coterminal0
   c. Undefined
   d. Undefined

120. The _____ is a property of multiplication or addition where the product or sum remains the same, regardless of whether or not the order of the addends or factors are changed.
   a. Thing
   b. Commutative property0
   c. Undefined
   d. Undefined

121. A _____ is one of the basic shapes of geometry: a polygon with three vertices and three sides which are straight line segments.
   a. Triangle0
   b. Thing
   c. Undefined
   d. Undefined

122. In mathematics, a _____ function in the sense of algebraic geometry is an everywhere-defined, polynomial function on an algebraic variety V with values in the field K over which V is defined.
   a. Regular0
   b. Thing
   c. Undefined
   d. Undefined

123. A _____ is a polygon with six edges and six vertices.
   a. Hexagon0
   b. Thing
   c. Undefined
   d. Undefined

124. In geometry, a _____ is any five-sided polygon.
   a. Thing
   b. Pentagon0
   c. Undefined
   d. Undefined

125. U.S. liquid _____ is legally defined as 231 cubic inches, and is equal to 3.785411784 litres or abotu 0.13368 cubic feet. This is the most common definition of a _____. The U.S. fluid ounce is defined as 1/128 of a U.S. _____.
a. Gallon0
b. Thing
c. Undefined
d. Undefined

126. _____ is the transport of people on a trip/journey or the process or time involved in a person or object moving from one location to another.
a. Travel0
b. Thing
c. Undefined
d. Undefined

127. In mathematics, an _____, mean, or central tendency of a data set refers to a measure of the "middle" or "expected" value of the data set.
a. Concept
b. Average0
c. Undefined
d. Undefined

128. In Euclidean geometry, a _____ is the set of all points in a plane at a fixed distance, called the radius, from a given point, the center.
a. Circle0
b. Thing
c. Undefined
d. Undefined

129. The _____ is the distance around a closed curve. _____ is a kind of perimeter.
a. Thing
b. Circumference0
c. Undefined
d. Undefined

130. A _____ is a compensation which workers receive in exchange for their labor.
a. Wage0
b. Thing
c. Undefined
d. Undefined

131. _____ is a state located in the southern and southwestern regions of the United States of America.
a. Texas0
b. Thing
c. Undefined
d. Undefined

132. A _____ is a consumption tax charged at the point of purchase for certain goods and services.
a. Thing
b. Sales tax0
c. Undefined
d. Undefined

133. _____ is a state located in the Midwestern region of the United States of America.
a. Thing
b. Minnesota0
c. Undefined
d. Undefined

134. _____ is a business term for the amount of money that a company receives from its activities in a given period, mostly from sales of products and/or services to customers
a. Thing
b. Revenue0
c. Undefined
d. Undefined

Chapter 1. Operations with Real Numbers

135. In mathematics, a _____ is the end result of a division problem. It can also be expressed as the number of times the divisor divides into the dividend.
 a. Quotient0
 b. Thing
 c. Undefined
 d. Undefined

136. In mathematics, a _____ of an integer n, also called a factor of n, is an integer which evenly divides n without leaving a remainder.
 a. Thing
 b. Divisor0
 c. Undefined
 d. Undefined

137. In mathematics, defined and _____ are used to explain whether or not expressions have meaningful, sensible, and unambiguous values.
 a. Undefined0
 b. Thing
 c. Undefined
 d. Undefined

138. _____ is the largest positive integer that divides both numbers without remainder.
 a. Thing
 b. Common Factor0
 c. Undefined
 d. Undefined

139. In mathematics, _____ expressions is used to reduce the expression into the lowest possible term.
 a. Thing
 b. Simplifying0
 c. Undefined
 d. Undefined

140. In the mathematical field of numerical analysis, the _____ in some data is the discrepancy between an exact value and some approximation to it.
 a. Thing
 b. Approximation Error0
 c. Undefined
 d. Undefined

141. The decimal separator is a symbol used to mark the boundary between the integral and the fractional parts of a decimal numeral. Terms implying the symbol used are _____ and decimal comma.
 a. Decimal point0
 b. Concept
 c. Undefined
 d. Undefined

142. The metre (or _____, see spelling differences) is a measure of length. It is the basic unit of length in the metric system and in the International System of Units (SI), used around the world for general and scientific purposes.
 a. Meter0
 b. Concept
 c. Undefined
 d. Undefined

143. In mathematics, the _____ of a function is the set of all "output" values produced by that function. Given a function $f : A \to B$, the _____ of f, is defined to be the set $\{x \in B : x = f(a) \text{ for some } a \in A\}$.
 a. Range0
 b. Thing
 c. Undefined
 d. Undefined

144. _____ is a mathematical science pertaining to the collection, analysis, interpretation or explanation, and presentation of data. It is applicable to a wide variety of academic disciplines, from the physical and social sciences to the humanities.

a. Thing
b. Statistics0
c. Undefined
d. Undefined

145. A _____ is a function that assigns a number to subsets of a given set.
a. Thing
b. Measure0
c. Undefined
d. Undefined

146. Acid _____ ratio measures the ability of a company to use its near cash or quick assets to immediately extinguish its current liabilities.
a. Thing
b. Test0
c. Undefined
d. Undefined

147. _____ is the estimation of a physical quantity such as distance, energy, temperature, or time.
a. Measurement0
b. Thing
c. Undefined
d. Undefined

148. _____ is a mathematical operation, written a^n, involving two numbers, the base a and the exponent n.
a. Thing
b. Exponentiating0
c. Undefined
d. Undefined

149. _____ is a mathematical operation, written a^n, involving two numbers, the base a and the exponent n.
a. Thing
b. Exponentiation0
c. Undefined
d. Undefined

150. A _____ is a three-dimensional solid object bounded by six square faces, facets, or sides, with three meeting at each vertex.
a. Cube0
b. Thing
c. Undefined
d. Undefined

151. _____ has many meanings, most of which simply .
a. Power0
b. Thing
c. Undefined
d. Undefined

152. In mathematics, the conjugate _____ or adjoint matrix of an m-by-n matrix A with complex entries is the n-by-m matrix A* obtained from A by taking the transpose and then taking the complex conjugate of each entry.
a. Thing
b. Pairs0
c. Undefined
d. Undefined

153. In mathematics, and in particular in abstract algebra, the _____ is a property of binary operations that generalises the distributive law from elementary algebra.
a. Distributive property0
b. Thing
c. Undefined
d. Undefined

154. In mathematics, _____ is the decomposition of an object into a product of other objects, or factors, which when multiplied together give the original.

Chapter 1. Operations with Real Numbers   17

a. Thing
b. Factoring0
c. Undefined
d. Undefined

155.   In mathematics, a _____ is a constant multiplicative factor of a certain object. The object can be such things as a variable, a vector, a function, etc. For example, the _____ of $9x^2$ is 9.
a. Coefficient0
b. Thing
c. Undefined
d. Undefined

156.   In mathematics, _____ growth occurs when the growth rate of a function is always proportional to the function's current size.
a. Exponential0
b. Thing
c. Undefined
d. Undefined

157.   In mathematics, a _____ is the set of all points in three-dimensional space (R^3) which are at distance r from a fixed point of that space, where r is a positive real number called the radius of the _____. The fixed point is called the center or centre, and is not part of the _____ itself.
a. Thing
b. Sphere0
c. Undefined
d. Undefined

158.   _____ is a set, with some particular properties and usually some additional structure, such as the operations of addition or multiplication, for instance.
a. Space0
b. Thing
c. Undefined
d. Undefined

159.   In mathematics, a _____ is a quadric surface, with the following equation in Cartesian coordinates: $(x/_a)^2 + (y/_b)^2 = 1$.
a. Cylinder0
b. Thing
c. Undefined
d. Undefined

160.   _____ is the application of tools and a processing medium to the transformation of raw materials into finished goods for sale.
a. Thing
b. Manufacturing0
c. Undefined
d. Undefined

161.   A _____ is an individual or company including a corporation that legally owns one or more shares of stock in a joint stock company.
a. Thing
b. Stockholder0
c. Undefined
d. Undefined

162.   Recurring or _____ are numbers which when expressed as decimals have a set of "final" digits which repeat an infinite number of times.
a. Repeating decimals0
b. Thing
c. Undefined
d. Undefined

163.   _____ represent rational numbers whose fractions in lowest terms are of the form $k/(2^n 5^m)$.

Chapter 1. Operations with Real Numbers

a. Thing
b. Terminating Decimals0
c. Undefined
d. Undefined

164. A _____ is a set whose members are members of another set or a set contained within another set.
a. Subset0
b. Thing
c. Undefined
d. Undefined

165. _____ are groups whose members are members of another set or a set contained within another set.
a. Subsets0
b. Thing
c. Undefined
d. Undefined

166. _____ is a notation for writing numbers that is often used by scientists and mathematicians to make it easier to write large and small numbers.
a. Thing
b. Scientific notation0
c. Undefined
d. Undefined

167. In mathematics, a matrix can be thought of as each row or _____ being a vector. Hence, a space formed by row vectors or _____ vectors are said to be a row space or a _____ space.
a. Concept
b. Column0
c. Undefined
d. Undefined

168. _____ is a sequence of numbers such that the difference of any two successive members of the sequence is a constant.
a. Arithmetic sequence0
b. Thing
c. Undefined
d. Undefined

169. _____ over a given field is a polynomial with coefficients in that field.
a. Thing
b. Algebraic equation0
c. Undefined
d. Undefined

170. A _____ is a deliberate process for transforming one or more inputs into one or more results.
a. Calculation0
b. Thing
c. Undefined
d. Undefined

171. _____ are activities that are governed by a set of rules or customs and often engaged in competitively.
a. Sports0
b. Thing
c. Undefined
d. Undefined

172. In chemistry, a _____ is substance made by combining two or more different materials in such a way that no chemical reaction occurs.
a. Mixture0
b. Thing
c. Undefined
d. Undefined

Chapter 2. Linear Equations and Patterns

1. A _____ is a type of debt. All material things can be lent but this article focuses exclusively on monetary loans. Like all debt instruments, a _____ entails the redistribution of financial assets over time, between the lender and the borrower.
    a. Loan0
    b. Thing
    c. Undefined
    d. Undefined

2. In mathematics, a _____ is an ordered list of objects. Like a set, it contains members, also called elements or terms, and the number of terms is called the length of the _____. Unlike a set, order matters, and the exact same elements can appear multiple times at different positions in the _____.
    a. Thing
    b. Sequence0
    c. Undefined
    d. Undefined

3. A _____ is a set of numbers that designate location in a given reference system, such as x,y in a planar _____ system or an x,y,z in a three-dimensional _____ system.
    a. Thing
    b. Coordinate0
    c. Undefined
    d. Undefined

4. In mathematics and its applications, a _____ is a system for assigning an n-tuple of numbers or scalars to each point in an n-dimensional space.
    a. Coordinate system0
    b. Concept
    c. Undefined
    d. Undefined

5. _____ or arithmetics is the oldest and most elementary branch of mathematics, used by almost everyone, for tasks ranging from simple daily counting to advanced science and business calculations.
    a. Thing
    b. Arithmetic0
    c. Undefined
    d. Undefined

6. _____ is a sequence of numbers such that the difference of any two successive members of the sequence is a constant.
    a. Thing
    b. Arithmetic sequence0
    c. Undefined
    d. Undefined

7. An _____ is a collection of two not necessarily distinct objects, one of which is distinguished as the first coordinate and the other as the second coordinate.
    a. Thing
    b. Ordered pair0
    c. Undefined
    d. Undefined

8. In mathematics, the conjugate _____ or adjoint matrix of an m-by-n matrix A with complex entries is the n-by-m matrix A* obtained from A by taking the transpose and then taking the complex conjugate of each entry.
    a. Pairs0
    b. Thing
    c. Undefined
    d. Undefined

9. In mathematics and the mathematical sciences, a _____ is a fixed, but possibly unspecified, value. This is in contrast to a variable, which is not fixed.
    a. Constant0
    b. Thing
    c. Undefined
    d. Undefined

10. A _____ is a one-dimensional picture in which the integers are shown as specially-marked points evenly spaced on a line.
   a. Thing
   b. Number line0
   c. Undefined
   d. Undefined

11. In mathematics, the _____ of a coordinate system is the point where the axes of the system intersect.
   a. Thing
   b. Origin0
   c. Undefined
   d. Undefined

12. In astronomy, geography, geometry and related sciences and contexts, a plane is said to be _____ at a given point if it is locally perpendicular to the gradient of the gravity field, i.e., with the direction of the gravitational force at that point.
   a. Horizontal0
   b. Thing
   c. Undefined
   d. Undefined

13. _____ is a branch of mathematics concerning the study of structure, relation and quantity.
   a. Algebra0
   b. Concept
   c. Undefined
   d. Undefined

14. _____ was a highly influential French philosopher, mathematician, scientist, and writer. Dubbed the "Founder of Modern Philosophy", and the "Father of Modern Mathematics". His theories provided the basis for the calculus of Newton and Leibniz, by applying infinitesimal calculus to the tangent line problem, thus permitting the evolution of that branch of modern mathematics
   a. Person
   b. Descartes0
   c. Undefined
   d. Undefined

15. In mathematics, a _____ is a two-dimensional manifold or surface that is perfectly flat.
   a. Thing
   b. Plane0
   c. Undefined
   d. Undefined

16. _____ has many meanings, most of which simply .
   a. Power0
   b. Thing
   c. Undefined
   d. Undefined

17. A _____ consists of one quarter of the coordinate plane.
   a. Thing
   b. Quadrant0
   c. Undefined
   d. Undefined

18. In geometry, a line _____ is a part of a line that is bounded by two end points, and contains every point on the line between its end points.
   a. Segment0
   b. Concept
   c. Undefined
   d. Undefined

19. In geometry, a _____ is defined as a quadrilateral where all four of its angles are right angles.
   a. Thing
   b. Rectangle0
   c. Undefined
   d. Undefined

Chapter 2. Linear Equations and Patterns

20. _____, either of the curved-bracket punctuation marks that together make a set of _____
    a. Thing
    b. Parentheses0
    c. Undefined
    d. Undefined

21. In elementary algebra, an _____ is a set that contains every real number between two indicated numbers and may contain the two numbers themselves.
    a. Thing
    b. Interval0
    c. Undefined
    d. Undefined

22. The _____ of measurement are a globally standardized and modernized form of the metric system.
    a. Units0
    b. Thing
    c. Undefined
    d. Undefined

23. An _____ is a combination of numbers, operators, grouping symbols and/or free variables and bound variables arranged in a meaningful way which can be evaluated..
    a. Thing
    b. Expression0
    c. Undefined
    d. Undefined

24. _____ is a synonym for information.
    a. Data0
    b. Thing
    c. Undefined
    d. Undefined

25. A _____ is a simplified and structured visual representation of concepts, ideas, constructions, relations, statistical data, anatomy etc used in all aspects of human activities to visualize and clarify the topic.
    a. Diagram0
    b. Thing
    c. Undefined
    d. Undefined

26. An _____ is a straight line around which a geometric figure can be rotated.
    a. Thing
    b. Axis0
    c. Undefined
    d. Undefined

27. In Euclidean geometry, a uniform _____ is a linear transformation that enlargers or diminishes objects, and whose _____ factor is the same in all directions. This is also called homothethy.
    a. Thing
    b. Scale0
    c. Undefined
    d. Undefined

28. The word _____ comes from the Latin word linearis, which means created by lines.
    a. Linear0
    b. Thing
    c. Undefined
    d. Undefined

29. Initial objects are also called _____, and terminal objects are also called final.
    a. Coterminal0
    b. Thing
    c. Undefined
    d. Undefined

30. _____ is a kind of property which exists as magnitude or multitude. It is among the basic classes of things along with quality, substance, change, and relation.

a. Amount0
b. Thing
c. Undefined
d. Undefined

31. In mathematics, in the field of differential equations, an initial value problem is a differential equation together with specified value, called the _____, of the unknown function at a given point in the domain of the solution.
   a. Initial condition0
   b. Thing
   c. Undefined
   d. Undefined

32. _____ means in succession or back-to-back
   a. Consecutive0
   b. Thing
   c. Undefined
   d. Undefined

33. An _____ is when two lines intersect somewhere on a plane creating a right angle at intersection
   a. Axes0
   b. Thing
   c. Undefined
   d. Undefined

34. _____ are activities that are governed by a set of rules or customs and often engaged in competitively.
   a. Sports0
   b. Thing
   c. Undefined
   d. Undefined

35. A _____ is an equation in which each term is either a constant or the product of a constant times the first power of a variable.
   a. Linear equation0
   b. Thing
   c. Undefined
   d. Undefined

36. In mathematics, an _____ is a statement about the relative size or order of two objects.
   a. Inequality0
   b. Thing
   c. Undefined
   d. Undefined

37. Mathematical _____ is used to represent ideas.
   a. Thing
   b. Notation0
   c. Undefined
   d. Undefined

38. A _____ is a first degree polynomial mathematical function of the form: $f(x) = mx + b$ where m and b are real constants and x is a real variable.
   a. Linear function0
   b. Thing
   c. Undefined
   d. Undefined

39. In banking and accountancy, the outstanding _____ is the amount of money owned, or due, that remains in a deposit account or a loan account at a given date, after all past remittances, payments and withdrawal have been accounted for.
   a. Thing
   b. Balance0
   c. Undefined
   d. Undefined

Chapter 2. Linear Equations and Patterns

40. The mathematical concept of a _____ expresses the intuitive idea of deterministic dependence between two quantities, one of which is viewed as primary and the other as secondary. A _____ then is a way to associate a unique output for each input of a specified type, for example, a real number or an element of a given set.
    a. Thing
    b. Function0
    c. Undefined
    d. Undefined

41. The _____, the average in everyday English, which is also called the arithmetic _____ (and is distinguished from the geometric _____ or harmonic _____). The average is also called the sample _____. The expected value of a random variable, which is also called the population _____.
    a. Thing
    b. Mean0
    c. Undefined
    d. Undefined

42. A _____ function is a function for which, intuitively, small changes in the input result in small changes in the output.
    a. Continuous0
    b. Event
    c. Undefined
    d. Undefined

43. In mathematics, a _____ may be described informally as a number that can be given by an infinite decimal representation.
    a. Real number0
    b. Thing
    c. Undefined
    d. Undefined

44. A _____ of a number is the product of that number with any integer.
    a. Thing
    b. Multiple0
    c. Undefined
    d. Undefined

45. The word _____ comes from the 15th Century Latin word discretus which means separate.
    a. Thing
    b. Discrete0
    c. Undefined
    d. Undefined

46. The plus and _____ signs are mathematical symbols used to represent the notions of positive and negative as well as the operations of addition and subtraction.
    a. Thing
    b. Minus0
    c. Undefined
    d. Undefined

47. A _____ is a symbolic representation denoting a quantity or expression. It often represents an "unknown" quantity that has the potential to change.
    a. Variable0
    b. Thing
    c. Undefined
    d. Undefined

48. In finance and economics, _____ is the process of finding the present value of an amount of cash at some future date, and along with compounding cash forms the basis of time value of money calculations.
    a. Discount0
    b. Thing
    c. Undefined
    d. Undefined

Chapter 2. Linear Equations and Patterns

49. A _____ is a special kind of ratio, indicating a relationship between two measurements with different units, such as miles to gallons or cents to pounds.
   a. Rate0
   b. Thing
   c. Undefined
   d. Undefined

50. A _____ is a unit of length, usually used to measure distance, in a number of different systems, including Imperial units, United States customary units and Norwegian/Swedish mil. Its size can vary from system to system, but in each is between 1 and 10 kilometers. In contemporary English contexts _____ refers to either:
   a. Thing
   b. Mile0
   c. Undefined
   d. Undefined

51. _____ is a unit of speed, expressing the number of international miles covered per hour.
   a. Miles per hour0
   b. Thing
   c. Undefined
   d. Undefined

52. _____ is the distance around a given two-dimensional object. As a general rule, the _____ of a polygon can always be calculated by adding all the length of the sides together. So, the formula for triangles is P = a + b + c, where a, b and c stand for each side of it. For quadrilaterals the equation is P = a + b + c + d. For equilateral polygons, P = na, where n is the number of sides and a is the side length.
   a. Thing
   b. Perimeter0
   c. Undefined
   d. Undefined

53. In business, _____, _____ cost or _____ expense refers to an ongoing expense of operating a business.
   a. Thing
   b. Overhead0
   c. Undefined
   d. Undefined

54. _____ are the basic objects of study in graph theory. Informally speaking, a graph is a set of objects called points, nodes, or vertices connected by links called lines or edges.
   a. Graphs0
   b. Thing
   c. Undefined
   d. Undefined

55. A _____ is a negotiable instrument instructing a financial institution to pay a specific amount of a specific currency from a specific demand account held in the maker/depositor's name with that institution. Both the maker and payee may be natural persons or legal entities.
   a. Thing
   b. Check0
   c. Undefined
   d. Undefined

56. In common philosophical language, a proposition or _____, is the content of an assertion, that is, it is true-or-false and defined by the meaning of a particular piece of language.
   a. Concept
   b. Statement0
   c. Undefined
   d. Undefined

57. _____ is the state of being greater than any finite real or natural number, however large.

Chapter 2. Linear Equations and Patterns

a. Infinite0
b. Thing
c. Undefined
d. Undefined

58. In set theory, an _____ is a set that is not a finite set. Infinite sets may be countable or uncountable.
    a. Thing
    b. Infinite set0
    c. Undefined
    d. Undefined

59. Any point where a graph makes contact with an coordinate axis is called an _____ of the graph
    a. Intercept0
    b. Thing
    c. Undefined
    d. Undefined

60. _____, from Latin meaning "to make progress", is defined in two different ways. Pure economic _____ is the increase in wealth that an investor has from making an investment, taking into consideration all costs associated with that investment including the opportunity cost of capital.
    a. Profit0
    b. Thing
    c. Undefined
    d. Undefined

61. In mathematics, the _____ of two sets A and B is the set that contains all elements of A that also belong to B (or equivalently, all elements of B that also belong to A), but no other elements.
    a. Intersection0
    b. Thing
    c. Undefined
    d. Undefined

62. _____ is the calculated approximation of a result which is usable even if input data may be incomplete, uncertain, or noisy.
    a. Concept
    b. Estimation0
    c. Undefined
    d. Undefined

63. In geographic information systems, a _____ comprises an entity with a geographic location, typically determined by points, arcs, or polygons. Carriageways and cadastres exemplify _____ data.
    a. Thing
    b. Feature0
    c. Undefined
    d. Undefined

64. In mathematics, factorization (British English: factorisation) or factoring is the decomposition of an object (for example, a number, a polynomial, or a matrix) into a product of other objects, or _____, which when multiplied together give the original.
    a. Factors0
    b. Thing
    c. Undefined
    d. Undefined

65. Equivalence is the condition of being _____ or essentially equal.
    a. Thing
    b. Equivalent0
    c. Undefined
    d. Undefined

66. _____ the expected value of a random variable displays the average or central value of the variable. It is a summary value of the distribution of the variable.

Chapter 2. Linear Equations and Patterns

    a. Determining0
    b. Thing
    c. Undefined
    d. Undefined

67. _____ is the study of error, particularly in the fields of applied mathematics, applied linguistics, statistics, and numerical analysis.
    a. Thing
    b. Error analysis0
    c. Undefined
    d. Undefined

68. In mathematics, there are several meanings of _____ depending on the subject.
    a. Degree0
    b. Thing
    c. Undefined
    d. Undefined

69. _____ , generally known as Franciscus Vieta, was a French mathematician.
    a. Person
    b. Francois Viete0
    c. Undefined
    d. Undefined

70. A _____ signifies a point or points of probability on a subject e.g., the _____ of creativity, which allows for the formation of rule or norm or law by interpretation of the phenomena events that can be created.
    a. Principle0
    b. Thing
    c. Undefined
    d. Undefined

71. A _____ is a set of possible values that a variable can take on in order to satisfy a given set of conditions, which may include equations and inequalities.
    a. Solution set0
    b. Thing
    c. Undefined
    d. Undefined

72. _____ element of an element x with respect to a binary operation * with identity element e is an element y such that x * y = y * x = e. In particular,
    a. Thing
    b. Inverse0
    c. Undefined
    d. Undefined

73. In mathematics, the _____ inverse, or opposite, of a number n is the number that, when added to n, yields zero. The _____ inverse of n is denoted −n.
    a. Thing
    b. Additive0
    c. Undefined
    d. Undefined

74. In mathematics, the _____ of a number n is the number that, when added to n, yields zero. The _____ of n is denoted −n. For example, 7 is −7, because 7 + (−7) = 0, and the _____ of −0.3 is 0.3, because −0.3 + 0.3 = 0.
    a. Thing
    b. Additive inverse0
    c. Undefined
    d. Undefined

75. Two mathematical objects are equal if and only if they are precisely the same in every way. This defines a binary relation, _____, denoted by the sign of _____ "=" in such a way that the statement "x = y" means that x and y are equal.

a. Equality0
b. Thing
c. Undefined
d. Undefined

76. _____ is a fixed, but possibly unspecified, value. This is in contrast to a variable, which is not fixed.
a. Constant term0
b. Thing
c. Undefined
d. Undefined

77. In mathematics, and in particular in abstract algebra, the _____ is a property of binary operations that generalises the distributive law from elementary algebra.
a. Thing
b. Distributive property0
c. Undefined
d. Undefined

78. The material _____, also known as the material implication or truth functional _____, expresses a property of certain conditionals in logic.
a. Thing
b. Conditional0
c. Undefined
d. Undefined

79. An _____ is an equality that remains true regardless of the values of any variables that appear within it, to distinguish it from an equality which is true under more particular conditions.
a. Identity0
b. Thing
c. Undefined
d. Undefined

80. Acid _____ ratio measures the ability of a company to use its near cash or quick assets to immediately extinguish its current liabilities.
a. Thing
b. Test0
c. Undefined
d. Undefined

81. Mathematical _____ are the wide variety of ways to capture an abstract mathematical concept or relationship.
a. Representations0
b. Thing
c. Undefined
d. Undefined

82. _____ over a given field is a polynomial with coefficients in that field.
a. Thing
b. Algebraic equation0
c. Undefined
d. Undefined

83. A _____ is the result of the addition of a set of numbers. The numbers may be natural numbers, complex numbers, matrices, or still more complicated objects. An infinite _____ is a subtle procedure known as a series.
a. Thing
b. Sum0
c. Undefined
d. Undefined

84. A _____ is one of the basic shapes of geometry: a polygon with three vertices and three sides which are straight line segments.
a. Triangle0
b. Thing
c. Undefined
d. Undefined

Chapter 2. Linear Equations and Patterns

85. _____ is bother the congnitive process of transferring information from a particular subject , and a linguistic expression corresponding to such a process.
   a. Analogy0
   b. Thing
   c. Undefined
   d. Undefined

86. The deductive-nomological model is a formalized view of scientific _____ in natural language.
   a. Explanation0
   b. Thing
   c. Undefined
   d. Undefined

87. In mathematics, _____ is an elementary arithmetic operation. When one of the numbers is a whole number, _____ is the repeated sum of the other number.
   a. Thing
   b. Multiplication0
   c. Undefined
   d. Undefined

88. In mathematics, a _____ is a constant multiplicative factor of a certain object. The object can be such things as a variable, a vector, a function, etc. For example, the _____ of $9x^2$ is 9.
   a. Coefficient0
   b. Thing
   c. Undefined
   d. Undefined

89. _____ variables are variables other than the independent variable that may bear any effect on the behavior of the subject being studied.
   a. Thing
   b. Extraneous0
   c. Undefined
   d. Undefined

90. In mathematics, the _____ inverse of a number x, denoted 1/x or x^{-1}, is the number which, when multiplied by x, yields 1. The _____ inverse of x is also called the reciprocal of x.
   a. Thing
   b. Multiplicative0
   c. Undefined
   d. Undefined

91. In mathematics, a _____ number is a number which can be expressed as a ratio of two integers. Non-integer _____ numbers (commonly called fractions) are usually written as the vulgar fraction a / b, where b is not zero.
   a. Thing
   b. Rational0
   c. Undefined
   d. Undefined

92. In mathematics, the multiplicative inverse of a number x, denoted 1/x or x^{-1}, is the number which, when multiplied by x, yields 1. The multiplicative inverse of x is also called the _____ of x.
   a. Reciprocal0
   b. Thing
   c. Undefined
   d. Undefined

93. A _____ is the part of a fraction that tells how many equal parts make up a whole, and which is used in the name of the fraction: "halves", "thirds", "fourths" or "quarters", "fifths" and so on.
   a. Concept
   b. Denominator0
   c. Undefined
   d. Undefined

94. In mathematics, a matrix can be thought of as each row or _____ being a vector. Hence, a space formed by row vectors or _____ vectors are said to be a row space or a _____ space.

Chapter 2. Linear Equations and Patterns

    a. Column0   b. Concept
    c. Undefined   d. Undefined

95. In plane geometry, a _____ is a polygon with four equal sides, four right angles, and parallel opposite sides. In algebra, the _____ of a number is that number multiplied by itself.
    a. Square0   b. Thing
    c. Undefined   d. Undefined

96. In geometry, an _____ polygon is a polygon which has all sides of the same length.
    a. Thing   b. Equilateral0
    c. Undefined   d. Undefined

97. An _____ is a triangle in which all sides are of equal length.
    a. Equilateral triangle0   b. Thing
    c. Undefined   d. Undefined

98. The metre (or _____, see spelling differences) is a measure of length. It is the basic unit of length in the metric system and in the International System of Units (SI), used around the world for general and scientific purposes.
    a. Meter0   b. Concept
    c. Undefined   d. Undefined

99. _____ (or proportionality) are two quantities that vary in such a way that one of the quatities is a constant multiple of the other, or equivalently if they have a constant ratio.
    a. Thing   b. Proportions0
    c. Undefined   d. Undefined

100. A _____ is a quantity that denotes the proportional amount or magnitude of one quantity relative to another.
    a. Thing   b. Ratio0
    c. Undefined   d. Undefined

101. A _____ is a four-sided plane figure that has two sets of opposite parallel sides.
    a. Parallelogram0   b. Concept
    c. Undefined   d. Undefined

102. In mathematics and logic, a _____ proof is a way of showing the truth or falsehood of a given statement by a straightforward combination of established facts, usually existing lemmas and theorems, without making any further assumptions.
    a. Thing   b. Direct0
    c. Undefined   d. Undefined

103. _____ is the relationship between two variables, like a ratio in which the two quantities being compared are different units.
    a. Thing   b. Direct variation0
    c. Undefined   d. Undefined

Chapter 2. Linear Equations and Patterns

104. A _____ is an abstract model that uses mathematical language to describe the behavior of a system. Eykhoff defined a _____ as 'a representation of the essential aspects of an existing system which presents knowledge of that system in usable form'.
- a. Thing
- b. Mathematical model0
- c. Undefined
- d. Undefined

105. _____ is a special mathematical relationship between two quantities. Two quantities are called proportional if they vary in such a way that one of the quantities is a constant multiple of the other, or equivalently if they have a constant ratio.
- a. Proportionality0
- b. Thing
- c. Undefined
- d. Undefined

106. In mathematics, an _____, mean, or central tendency of a data set refers to a measure of the "middle" or "expected" value of the data set.
- a. Average0
- b. Concept
- c. Undefined
- d. Undefined

107. In mathematics, two quantities are called _____ if they vary in such a way that one of the quantities is a constant multiple of the other, or equivalently if they have a constant ratio.
- a. Thing
- b. Proportional0
- c. Undefined
- d. Undefined

108. In mathematics, a _____ can mean either an element of the set {1, 2, 3, ...} (i.e the positive integers or the counting numbers) or an element of the set {0, 1, 2, 3, ...} (i.e. the non-negative integers).
- a. Thing
- b. Natural number0
- c. Undefined
- d. Undefined

109. _____ is the transport of people on a trip/journey or the process or time involved in a person or object moving from one location to another.
- a. Thing
- b. Travel0
- c. Undefined
- d. Undefined

110. The _____ of a solid object is the three-dimensional concept of how much space it occupies, often quantified numerically.
- a. Thing
- b. Volume0
- c. Undefined
- d. Undefined

111. _____ is a physical property of a system that underlies the common notions of hot and cold; something that is hotter has the greater _____.
- a. Temperature0
- b. Thing
- c. Undefined
- d. Undefined

112. A _____ is a function that assigns a number to subsets of a given set.
- a. Measure0
- b. Thing
- c. Undefined
- d. Undefined

Chapter 2. Linear Equations and Patterns

113. _____ is a concept in traditional logic referring to a "type of immediate inference in which from a given proposition another proposition is inferred which has as its subject the predicate of the original proposition and as its predicate the subject of the original proposition (the quality of the proposition being retained)."
   a. Concept
   b. Conversion0
   c. Undefined
   d. Undefined

114. In mathematics, _____ refers to the rewriting of an expression into a simpler form.
   a. Thing
   b. Reduction0
   c. Undefined
   d. Undefined

115. _____ is often used to describe the measurement of the steepness, incline, gradient, or grade of a straight line. The _____ is defined as the ratio of the "rise" divided by the "run" between two points on a line, or in other words, the ratio of the altitude change to the horizontal distance between any two points on the line.
   a. Thing
   b. Slope0
   c. Undefined
   d. Undefined

116. _____ is the estimation of a physical quantity such as distance, energy, temperature, or time.
   a. Thing
   b. Measurement0
   c. Undefined
   d. Undefined

117. A _____ is a deliberate process for transforming one or more inputs into one or more results.
   a. Thing
   b. Calculation0
   c. Undefined
   d. Undefined

118. _____ is the fee paid on borrowed money.
   a. Interest0
   b. Thing
   c. Undefined
   d. Undefined

119. An _____ is the fee paid on borrow money.
   a. Concept
   b. Interest rate0
   c. Undefined
   d. Undefined

120. Statistical _____ is a statistical procedure in which individual items are placed into groups based on quantitative information on one or more characteristics inherent in the items and based on a training set of previously labeled items.
   a. Classification0
   b. Thing
   c. Undefined
   d. Undefined

121. In linear algebra, the _____ of a matrix A is another matrix AT
   a. Thing
   b. Transpose0
   c. Undefined
   d. Undefined

122. In mathematics, the additive inverse, or _____ of a number n is the number that, when added to n, yields zero. The additive inverse of n is denoted −n. For example, 7 is −7, because 7 + (−7) = 0, and the additive inverse of −0.3 is 0.3, because −0.3 + 0.3 = 0.

a. Thing
b. Opposite0
c. Undefined
d. Undefined

123. A _____ is a three-dimensional geometric shape formed by straight lines through a fixed point (vertex) to the points of a fixed curve (directrix)
a. Cone0
b. Concept
c. Undefined
d. Undefined

124. _____ is a business term for the amount of money that a company receives from its activities in a given period, mostly from sales of products and/or services to customers
a. Revenue0
b. Thing
c. Undefined
d. Undefined

125. In business, particularly accounting, a _____ is the time intervals that the accounts, statement, payments, or other calculations cover.
a. Period0
b. Thing
c. Undefined
d. Undefined

Chapter 3. Lines and Systems of Linear Equations in Two Variables

1. A _____ is a special kind of ratio, indicating a relationship between two measurements with different units, such as miles to gallons or cents to pounds.
   a. Thing
   b. Rate0
   c. Undefined
   d. Undefined

2. _____ is the fee paid on borrowed money.
   a. Thing
   b. Interest0
   c. Undefined
   d. Undefined

3. An _____ is the fee paid on borrow money.
   a. Concept
   b. Interest rate0
   c. Undefined
   d. Undefined

4. The _____ of a geographic location is its height above a fixed reference point, often the mean sea level.
   a. Thing
   b. Elevation0
   c. Undefined
   d. Undefined

5. In mathematics, a subset of Euclidean space R^n is called _____ if it is closed and bounded.
   a. Thing
   b. Compact0
   c. Undefined
   d. Undefined

6. In probability theory, _____ are various sets of outcomes (a subset of the sample space) to which a probability is assigned.
   a. Events0
   b. Thing
   c. Undefined
   d. Undefined

7. _____ is often used to describe the measurement of the steepness, incline, gradient, or grade of a straight line. The _____ is defined as the ratio of the "rise" divided by the "run" between two points on a line, or in other words, the ratio of the altitude change to the horizontal distance between any two points on the line.
   a. Slope0
   b. Thing
   c. Undefined
   d. Undefined

8. In geometry, two lines or planes if one falls on the other in such a way as to create congruent adjacent angles. The term may be used as a noun or adjective. Thus, referring to Figure 1, the line AB is the _____ to CD through the point B.
   a. Perpendicular0
   b. Thing
   c. Undefined
   d. Undefined

9. _____ are the basic objects of study in graph theory. Informally speaking, a graph is a set of objects called points, nodes, or vertices connected by links called lines or edges.
   a. Graphs0
   b. Thing
   c. Undefined
   d. Undefined

10. An _____ is a straight line around which a geometric figure can be rotated.
    a. Thing
    b. Axis0
    c. Undefined
    d. Undefined

11. In Euclidean geometry, a uniform _____ is a linear transformation that enlargers or diminishes objects, and whose _____ factor is the same in all directions. This is also called homothethy.
   a. Thing
   b. Scale0
   c. Undefined
   d. Undefined

12. A _____ is a function that assigns a number to subsets of a given set.
   a. Measure0
   b. Thing
   c. Undefined
   d. Undefined

13. In mathematics, the _____ of a coordinate system is the point where the axes of the system intersect.
   a. Origin0
   b. Thing
   c. Undefined
   d. Undefined

14. A _____ is a landform that extends above the surrounding terrain in a limited area. A _____ is generally steeper than a hill, but there is no universally accepted standard definition for the height of a _____ or a hill although a _____ usually has an identifiable summit.
   a. Mountain0
   b. Thing
   c. Undefined
   d. Undefined

15. In Euclidean geometry, a _____ is the set of all points in a plane at a fixed distance, called the radius, from a given point, the center.
   a. Thing
   b. Circle0
   c. Undefined
   d. Undefined

16. _____ was an American mathematician, known for his work in geometry and the history of mathematics.
   a. Person
   b. Howard Eves0
   c. Undefined
   d. Undefined

17. _____, either of the curved-bracket punctuation marks that together make a set of _____
   a. Thing
   b. Parentheses0
   c. Undefined
   d. Undefined

18. _____ is the change in total cost that arises when the quantity produced changes by one unit.
   a. Marginal cost0
   b. Thing
   c. Undefined
   d. Undefined

19. An _____ is a combination of numbers, operators, grouping symbols and/or free variables and bound variables arranged in a meaningful way which can be evaluated..
   a. Expression0
   b. Thing
   c. Undefined
   d. Undefined

20. The _____ of measurement are a globally standardized and modernized form of the metric system.
   a. Units0
   b. Thing
   c. Undefined
   d. Undefined

21. A _____ is a number that is less than zero.

a. Thing
b. Negative number0
c. Undefined
d. Undefined

22. A _____ is a numeral used to indicate a count. The most common use of the word today is to name the part of a fraction that tells the number or count of equal parts.
   a. Numerator0
   b. Thing
   c. Undefined
   d. Undefined

23. A _____ is a quantity that denotes the proportional amount or magnitude of one quantity relative to another.
   a. Ratio0
   b. Thing
   c. Undefined
   d. Undefined

24. A _____ is a set of numbers that designate location in a given reference system, such as x,y in a planar _____ system or an x,y,z in a three-dimensional _____ system.
   a. Coordinate0
   b. Thing
   c. Undefined
   d. Undefined

25. In mathematics and its applications, a _____ is a system for assigning an n-tuple of numbers or scalars to each point in an n-dimensional space.
   a. Coordinate system0
   b. Concept
   c. Undefined
   d. Undefined

26. The _____ of a mathematical object is its size: a property by which it can be larger or smaller than other objects of the same kind; in technical terms, an ordering of the class of objects to which it belongs.
   a. Thing
   b. Magnitude0
   c. Undefined
   d. Undefined

27. In mathematics, defined and _____ are used to explain whether or not expressions have meaningful, sensible, and unambiguous values.
   a. Thing
   b. Undefined0
   c. Undefined
   d. Undefined

28. In astronomy, geography, geometry and related sciences and contexts, a plane is said to be _____ at a given point if it is locally perpendicular to the gradient of the gravity field, i.e., with the direction of the gravitational force at that point.
   a. Thing
   b. Horizontal0
   c. Undefined
   d. Undefined

29. A _____ is a negotiable instrument instructing a financial institution to pay a specific amount of a specific currency from a specific demand account held in the maker/depositor's name with that institution. Both the maker and payee may be natural persons or legal entities.
   a. Check0
   b. Thing
   c. Undefined
   d. Undefined

30. In mathematics, a _____ is an ordered list of objects. Like a set, it contains members, also called elements or terms, and the number of terms is called the length of the _____. Unlike a set, order matters, and the exact same elements can appear multiple times at different positions in the _____.

Chapter 3. Lines and Systems of Linear Equations in Two Variables

    a. Sequence0
    c. Undefined
    b. Thing
    d. Undefined

31. _____ or arithmetics is the oldest and most elementary branch of mathematics, used by almost everyone, for tasks ranging from simple daily counting to advanced science and business calculations.
    a. Thing
    b. Arithmetic0
    c. Undefined
    d. Undefined

32. _____ is a sequence of numbers such that the difference of any two successive members of the sequence is a constant.
    a. Arithmetic sequence0
    b. Thing
    c. Undefined
    d. Undefined

33. The word _____ comes from the Latin word linearis, which means created by lines.
    a. Thing
    b. Linear0
    c. Undefined
    d. Undefined

34. _____ means in succession or back-to-back
    a. Thing
    b. Consecutive0
    c. Undefined
    d. Undefined

35. A _____ is a symbolic representation denoting a quantity or expression. It often represents an "unknown" quantity that has the potential to change.
    a. Thing
    b. Variable0
    c. Undefined
    d. Undefined

36. The existence and properties of _____ are the basis of Euclid's parallel postulate. _____ are two lines on the same plane that do not intersect even assuming that lines extend to infinity in either direction.
    a. Parallel lines0
    b. Thing
    c. Undefined
    d. Undefined

37. In mathematics, a _____ is a two-dimensional manifold or surface that is perfectly flat.
    a. Plane0
    b. Thing
    c. Undefined
    d. Undefined

38. In mathematics, the multiplicative inverse of a number x, denoted $1/x$ or x^{-1}, is the number which, when multiplied by x, yields 1. The multiplicative inverse of x is also called the _____ of x.
    a. Reciprocal0
    b. Thing
    c. Undefined
    d. Undefined

39. In mathematics, the additive inverse, or _____ of a number n is the number that, when added to n, yields zero. The additive inverse of n is denoted −n. For example, 7 is −7, because 7 + (−7) = 0, and the additive inverse of −0.3 is 0.3, because −0.3 + 0.3 = 0.
    a. Opposite0
    b. Thing
    c. Undefined
    d. Undefined

Chapter 3. Lines and Systems of Linear Equations in Two Variables

40. In mathematics, the _____ of a number n is the number that, when added to n, yields zero. The _____ of n is denoted −n. For example, 7 is −7, because 7 + (−7) = 0, and the _____ of −0.3 is 0.3, because −0.3 + 0.3 = 0.
   a. Thing
   b. Additive inverse0
   c. Undefined
   d. Undefined

41. In mathematics, a _____ is the result of multiplying, or an expression that identifies factors to be multiplied.
   a. Product0
   b. Thing
   c. Undefined
   d. Undefined

42. _____ is the calculated approximation of a result which is usable even if input data may be incomplete, uncertain, or noisy.
   a. Estimation0
   b. Concept
   c. Undefined
   d. Undefined

43. In mathematics, the conjugate _____ or adjoint matrix of an m-by-n matrix A with complex entries is the n-by-m matrix A* obtained from A by taking the transpose and then taking the complex conjugate of each entry.
   a. Pairs0
   b. Thing
   c. Undefined
   d. Undefined

44. In geometry, a _____ is the intersection of a body in 2-dimensional space with a line, or of a body in 3-dimensional space with a plane
   a. Thing
   b. Cross section0
   c. Undefined
   d. Undefined

45. A _____ is an equation in which each term is either a constant or the product of a constant times the first power of a variable.
   a. Thing
   b. Linear equation0
   c. Undefined
   d. Undefined

46. _____ is a synonym for information.
   a. Thing
   b. Data0
   c. Undefined
   d. Undefined

47. The _____ (symbol _____) and the millibar (symbol mbar, also mb) are units of pressure.
   a. Bar0
   b. Thing
   c. Undefined
   d. Undefined

48. _____ is the study of terms and their use — of words and compound words that are used in specific contexts.
   a. Thing
   b. Terminology0
   c. Undefined
   d. Undefined

49. Mathematical _____ are the wide variety of ways to capture an abstract mathematical concept or relationship.
   a. Thing
   b. Representations0
   c. Undefined
   d. Undefined

50. _____ the expected value of a random variable displays the average or central value of the variable. It is a summary value of the distribution of the variable.
- a. Determining0
- b. Thing
- c. Undefined
- d. Undefined

51. One of the three formats applicable to a quadratic function is the _____ which is defined as $f = ax^2 + bx + c$.
- a. Thing
- b. General form0
- c. Undefined
- d. Undefined

52. In mathematics, a _____ may be described informally as a number that can be given by an infinite decimal representation.
- a. Thing
- b. Real number0
- c. Undefined
- d. Undefined

53. The _____, the average in everyday English, which is also called the arithmetic _____ (and is distinguished from the geometric _____ or harmonic _____). The average is also called the sample _____. The expected value of a random variable, which is also called the population _____.
- a. Mean0
- b. Thing
- c. Undefined
- d. Undefined

54. A _____ is the part of a fraction that tells how many equal parts make up a whole, and which is used in the name of the fraction: "halves", "thirds", "fourths" or "quarters", "fifths" and so on.
- a. Denominator0
- b. Concept
- c. Undefined
- d. Undefined

55. In mathematics, a _____ is a constant multiplicative factor of a certain object. The object can be such things as a variable, a vector, a function, etc. For example, the _____ of $9x^2$ is 9.
- a. Coefficient0
- b. Thing
- c. Undefined
- d. Undefined

56. _____ is a form of periodic payment from an employer to an employee, which is specified in an employment contract.
- a. Thing
- b. Gross pay0
- c. Undefined
- d. Undefined

57. A _____ is a form of periodic payment from an employer to an employee, which is specified in an employment contract.
- a. Thing
- b. Salary0
- c. Undefined
- d. Undefined

58. _____ is a payment made by a company to its shareholders
- a. Dividend0
- b. Thing
- c. Undefined
- d. Undefined

59. The payment of _____ as remuneration for services rendered or products sold is a common way to reward sales people.

Chapter 3. Lines and Systems of Linear Equations in Two Variables

a. Thing
b. Commission0
c. Undefined
d. Undefined

60. The _____ or kilogramme is the SI base unit of mass. It is defined as being equal to the mass of the international prototype of the _____.
a. Thing
b. Kilogram0
c. Undefined
d. Undefined

61. _____ is the property of a physical object that quantifies the amount of matter and energy it is equivalent to.
a. Thing
b. Mass0
c. Undefined
d. Undefined

62. _____, from Latin meaning "to make progress", is defined in two different ways. Pure economic _____ is the increase in wealth that an investor has from making an investment, taking into consideration all costs associated with that investment including the opportunity cost of capital.
a. Profit0
b. Thing
c. Undefined
d. Undefined

63. In economics, economic _____ is simply a state of the world where economic forces are balanced and in the absence of external influences the values of economic variables will not change.
a. Thing
b. Equilibrium0
c. Undefined
d. Undefined

64. In business, particularly accounting, a _____ is the time intervals that the accounts, statement, payments, or other calculations cover.
a. Period0
b. Thing
c. Undefined
d. Undefined

65. An _____ is a collection of two not necessarily distinct objects, one of which is distinguished as the first coordinate and the other as the second coordinate.
a. Ordered pair0
b. Thing
c. Undefined
d. Undefined

66. In mathematics, the _____ of two sets A and B is the set that contains all elements of A that also belong to B (or equivalently, all elements of B that also belong to A), but no other elements.
a. Thing
b. Intersection0
c. Undefined
d. Undefined

67. _____ is the state of being greater than any finite real or natural number, however large.
a. Thing
b. Infinite0
c. Undefined
d. Undefined

68. Statistical _____ is a statistical procedure in which individual items are placed into groups based on quantitative information on one or more characteristics inherent in the items and based on a training set of previously labeled items.

a. Thing
b. Classification0
c. Undefined
d. Undefined

69. In geometry, a _____ is defined as a quadrilateral where all four of its angles are right angles.
    a. Thing
    b. Rectangle0
    c. Undefined
    d. Undefined

70. In geographic information systems, a _____ comprises an entity with a geographic location, typically determined by points, arcs, or polygons. Carriageways and cadastres exemplify _____ data.
    a. Feature0
    b. Thing
    c. Undefined
    d. Undefined

71. The mathematical concept of a _____ expresses the intuitive idea of deterministic dependence between two quantities, one of which is viewed as primary and the other as secondary. A _____ then is a way to associate a unique output for each input of a specified type, for example, a real number or an element of a given set.
    a. Function0
    b. Thing
    c. Undefined
    d. Undefined

72. A pair of angles is _____ if their respective measures sum to 180 degrees.
    a. Concept
    b. Supplementary0
    c. Undefined
    d. Undefined

73. In mathematics, there are several meanings of _____ depending on the subject.
    a. Degree0
    b. Thing
    c. Undefined
    d. Undefined

74. A _____ is the result of the addition of a set of numbers. The numbers may be natural numbers, complex numbers, matrices, or still more complicated objects. An infinite _____ is a subtle procedure known as a series.
    a. Thing
    b. Sum0
    c. Undefined
    d. Undefined

75. A pair of angles are _____ if the sum of their angles is 90°.
    a. Complementary0
    b. Concept
    c. Undefined
    d. Undefined

76. Fixed costs are expenses whose total does not change in proportion to the activity of a business. Unit fixed costs decline with volume following a retangular hyperbola as the volume of production. Variable costs by contrast change in relation to the activity of a business such as sales or production volume. Along with variable costs, fixed costs make up one of the two components of total cost. In the most simple production function total cost is equal to fixed costs plus variable costs. In accounting terminology, fixed costs will broadly include all costs which are not included in cost of goods sold, and variable costs are those captured in costs of goods sold. The implicit assumption required to make the equivalence between the accounting and economics terminology is that the accounting period is equal to the period in which fixed costs do not vary in relation to production. In practice, this equivalence does not always hold and depending on the period under consideration by management, some overhead expenses can be adjusted by management, and the specific allocation of each expense to each category will be decided under cost accounting. In business planning and management accounting, usage of the terms fixed costs, variable costs and others will often differ from usage in economics, and may depend on the intended use. For example, costs may be segregated into per unit costs fixed costs per period, and variable costs as a proportion of revenue. Capital expenditures will usually be allocated separately, and depending on the purpose, a portion may be regularly allocated to expenses as depreciation and amortization and seen as a _____ per period, or the entire amount may be considered upfront fixed costs.
   a. Fixed cost0
   b. Thing
   c. Undefined
   d. Undefined

77. Mathematical _____ is used to represent ideas.
   a. Thing
   b. Notation0
   c. Undefined
   d. Undefined

78. A _____ is a unit of length, usually used to measure distance, in a number of different systems, including Imperial units, United States customary units and Norwegian/Swedish mil. Its size can vary from system to system, but in each is between 1 and 10 kilometers. In contemporary English contexts _____ refers to either:
   a. Thing
   b. Mile0
   c. Undefined
   d. Undefined

79. _____ is the transport of people on a trip/journey or the process or time involved in a person or object moving from one location to another.
   a. Travel0
   b. Thing
   c. Undefined
   d. Undefined

80. In botany, _____ are above-ground plant organs specialized for photosynthesis. Their characteristics are typically analyzed by using Fiobonacci's sequences.
   a. Leaves0
   b. Thing
   c. Undefined
   d. Undefined

81. A _____ of a number is the product of that number with any integer.
   a. Multiple0
   b. Thing
   c. Undefined
   d. Undefined

82. The _____ is used to discard one of the variables in an equation, only to replace it with the actual value when solving multiple equations.

Chapter 3. Lines and Systems of Linear Equations in Two Variables

   a. Substitution method0
   c. Undefined
   b. Thing
   d. Undefined

83. _____ systems represent systems whose behavior is not expressible as a sum of the behaviors of its descriptors.
   a. Thing
   c. Undefined
   b. Nonlinear0
   d. Undefined

84. A _____ represents a system whose behavior is not expressible as a sum of the behaviors of its descriptors.
   a. Thing
   c. Undefined
   b. Nonlinear system0
   d. Undefined

85. An _____ is an equality that remains true regardless of the values of any variables that appear within it, to distinguish it from an equality which is true under more particular conditions.
   a. Identity0
   c. Undefined
   b. Thing
   d. Undefined

86. In mathematics, an _____, mean, or central tendency of a data set refers to a measure of the "middle" or "expected" value of the data set.
   a. Average0
   c. Undefined
   b. Concept
   d. Undefined

87. Acid _____ ratio measures the ability of a company to use its near cash or quick assets to immediately extinguish its current liabilities.
   a. Thing
   c. Undefined
   b. Test0
   d. Undefined

88. In mathematics, the _____ of a function is the set of all "output" values produced by that function. Given a function $f : A \to B$, the _____ of f, is defined to be the set $\{x \in B : x = f(a) \text{ for some } a \in A\}$.
   a. Range0
   c. Undefined
   b. Thing
   d. Undefined

89. _____ is a branch of mathematics concerning the study of structure, relation and quantity.
   a. Algebra0
   c. Undefined
   b. Concept
   d. Undefined

90. _____ are objects, characters, or other concrete representations of ideas, concepts, or other abstractions.
   a. Symbols0
   c. Undefined
   b. Thing
   d. Undefined

91. A _____ signifies a point or points of probability on a subject e.g., the _____ of creativity, which allows for the formation of rule or norm or law by interpretation of the phenomena events that can be created.
   a. Thing
   c. Undefined
   b. Principle0
   d. Undefined

Chapter 3. Lines and Systems of Linear Equations in Two Variables 43

92. The _____ is focused on the substitution of a product, service or process to another that is more efficient or beneficial in some way while retaining the same functionality.
   a. Thing
   b. Substitution Principle0
   c. Undefined
   d. Undefined

93. The material _____, also known as the material implication or truth functional _____, expresses a property of certain conditionals in logic.
   a. Thing
   b. Conditional0
   c. Undefined
   d. Undefined

94. In sociology and biology a _____ is the collection of people or organisms of a particular species living in a given geographic area or space, usually measured by a census.
   a. Population0
   b. Thing
   c. Undefined
   d. Undefined

95. _____ is change in population over time, and can be quantified as the change in the number of individuals in a population per unit time.
   a. Thing
   b. Population growth0
   c. Undefined
   d. Undefined

96. In mathematics and the mathematical sciences, a _____ is a fixed, but possibly unspecified, value. This is in contrast to a variable, which is not fixed.
   a. Thing
   b. Constant0
   c. Undefined
   d. Undefined

97. _____ element of an element x with respect to a binary operation * with identity element e is an element y such that $x * y = y * x = e$. In particular,
   a. Thing
   b. Inverse0
   c. Undefined
   d. Undefined

98. In mathematics, the _____ inverse, or opposite, of a number n is the number that, when added to n, yields zero. The _____ inverse of n is denoted −n.
   a. Additive0
   b. Thing
   c. Undefined
   d. Undefined

99. A _____ fraction is a fraction in which the absolute value of the numerator is less than the denominator--hence, the absolute value of the fraction is less than 1.
   a. Proper0
   b. Thing
   c. Undefined
   d. Undefined

100. In banking and accountancy, the outstanding _____ is the amount of money owned, or due, that remains in a deposit account or a loan account at a given date, after all past remittances, payments and withdrawal have been accounted for.
   a. Balance0
   b. Thing
   c. Undefined
   d. Undefined

101. Two mathematical objects are equal if and only if they are precisely the same in every way. This defines a binary relation, _____, denoted by the sign of _____ "=" in such a way that the statement "x = y" means that x and y are equal.
   a. Equality0
   b. Thing
   c. Undefined
   d. Undefined

102. Equivalence is the condition of being _____ or essentially equal.
   a. Equivalent0
   b. Thing
   c. Undefined
   d. Undefined

103. The plus and _____ signs are mathematical symbols used to represent the notions of positive and negative as well as the operations of addition and subtraction.
   a. Minus0
   b. Thing
   c. Undefined
   d. Undefined

104. In geometry, the _____ of a vertex of a polyhedron is the amount by which the sum of the angles of the faces at the vertex falls short of a full circle.
   a. Thing
   b. Defect0
   c. Undefined
   d. Undefined

105. In geometry, a _____ (Greek words diairo = divide and metro = measure) of a circle is any straight line segment that passes through the centre and whose endpoints are on the circular boundary, or, in more modern usage, the length of such a line segment. When using the word in the more modern sense, one speaks of the _____ rather than a _____, because all diameters of a circle have the same length. This length is twice the radius. The _____ of a circle is also the longest chord that the circle has.
   a. Thing
   b. Diameter0
   c. Undefined
   d. Undefined

106. _____ is the estimation of a physical quantity such as distance, energy, temperature, or time.
   a. Thing
   b. Measurement0
   c. Undefined
   d. Undefined

107. _____ is a way of expressing a number as a fraction of 100 per cent meaning "per hundred".
   a. Percent0
   b. Thing
   c. Undefined
   d. Undefined

108. A _____ is the sum of the elements of a sequence.
   a. Series0
   b. Thing
   c. Undefined
   d. Undefined

109. _____ forms part of thinking. Considered the most complex of all intellectual functions, _____ has been defined as higher-order cognitive process that requires the modulation and control of more routine or fundamental skills.
   a. Thing
   b. Problem solving0
   c. Undefined
   d. Undefined

Chapter 3. Lines and Systems of Linear Equations in Two Variables

110. _____ is a kind of property which exists as magnitude or multitude. It is among the basic classes of things along with quality, substance, change, and relation.
   a. Amount0
   b. Thing
   c. Undefined
   d. Undefined

111. _____ over a given field is a polynomial with coefficients in that field.
   a. Algebraic equation0
   b. Thing
   c. Undefined
   d. Undefined

112. In chemistry, a _____ is substance made by combining two or more different materials in such a way that no chemical reaction occurs.
   a. Mixture0
   b. Thing
   c. Undefined
   d. Undefined

113. Multiple Signal Classification, also known as _____, is an algorithm used for frequency estimation and emitter location.
   a. Thing
   b. Music0
   c. Undefined
   d. Undefined

114. In commerce, a _____ is a party that mediates between a buyer and a seller.
   a. Broker0
   b. Thing
   c. Undefined
   d. Undefined

115. _____ or investing is a term with several closely-related meanings in business management, finance and economics, related to saving or deferring consumption.
   a. Thing
   b. Investment0
   c. Undefined
   d. Undefined

116. In topology and related areas of mathematics a _____ or Moore-Smith sequence is a generalization of a sequence, intended to unify the various notions of limit and generalize them to arbitrary topological spaces.
   a. Net0
   b. Thing
   c. Undefined
   d. Undefined

117. _____ are a measure of time.
   a. Thing
   b. Minutes0
   c. Undefined
   d. Undefined

118. In mathematics, an _____ is a statement about the relative size or order of two objects.
   a. Thing
   b. Inequality0
   c. Undefined
   d. Undefined

119. _____ is a physical property of a system that underlies the common notions of hot and cold; something that is hotter has the greater _____.
   a. Thing
   b. Temperature0
   c. Undefined
   d. Undefined

120. In physics, _____ is rotation along a circle: a circular path or a circular orbit. The rotation around a fixed axis of a three-dimensional body involves _____ of its parts. We can talk about _____ of an object if we ignore its size, so that we have the motion of a point mass in a plane.

a. Circular motion0
b. Thing
c. Undefined
d. Undefined

Chapter 4. Linear Inequalities and Systems of Linear Inequalities

1. In mathematics, an _____ is a statement about the relative size or order of two objects.
   a. Inequality0
   b. Thing
   c. Undefined
   d. Undefined

2. A _____ signifies a point or points of probability on a subject e.g., the _____ of creativity, which allows for the formation of rule or norm or law by interpretation of the phenomena events that can be created.
   a. Thing
   b. Principle0
   c. Undefined
   d. Undefined

3. A _____ is a negotiable instrument instructing a financial institution to pay a specific amount of a specific currency from a specific demand account held in the maker/depositor's name with that institution. Both the maker and payee may be natural persons or legal entities.
   a. Check0
   b. Thing
   c. Undefined
   d. Undefined

4. The word _____ comes from the Latin word linearis, which means created by lines.
   a. Thing
   b. Linear0
   c. Undefined
   d. Undefined

5. A _____ is a symbolic representation denoting a quantity or expression. It often represents an "unknown" quantity that has the potential to change.
   a. Variable0
   b. Thing
   c. Undefined
   d. Undefined

6. A _____ is an equation in which each term is either a constant or the product of a constant times the first power of a variable.
   a. Linear equation0
   b. Thing
   c. Undefined
   d. Undefined

7. The material _____, also known as the material implication or truth functional _____, expresses a property of certain conditionals in logic.
   a. Conditional0
   b. Thing
   c. Undefined
   d. Undefined

8. In mathematics and the mathematical sciences, a _____ is a fixed, but possibly unspecified, value. This is in contrast to a variable, which is not fixed.
   a. Thing
   b. Constant0
   c. Undefined
   d. Undefined

9. In geometry, an _____ is a point at which a line segment or ray terminates.
   a. Endpoint0
   b. Thing
   c. Undefined
   d. Undefined

10. In common philosophical language, a proposition or _____, is the content of an assertion, that is, it is true-or-false and defined by the meaning of a particular piece of language.

a. Concept
b. Statement0
c. Undefined
d. Undefined

11. _____ is the state of being greater than any finite real or natural number, however large.
a. Thing
b. Infinite0
c. Undefined
d. Undefined

12. In elementary algebra, an _____ is a set that contains every real number between two indicated numbers and may contain the two numbers themselves.
a. Thing
b. Interval0
c. Undefined
d. Undefined

13. Mathematical _____ is used to represent ideas.
a. Thing
b. Notation0
c. Undefined
d. Undefined

14. In mathematics, there are several meanings of _____ depending on the subject.
a. Degree0
b. Thing
c. Undefined
d. Undefined

15. _____ is the notation in which permitted values for a variable are expressed as ranging over a certain interval; "5 < x < 9" is an example of the application of _____.
a. Thing
b. Interval notation0
c. Undefined
d. Undefined

16. In mathematics, the _____ of two sets A and B is the set that contains all elements of A that also belong to B (or equivalently, all elements of B that also belong to A), but no other elements.
a. Intersection0
b. Thing
c. Undefined
d. Undefined

17. _____ is a fixed, but possibly unspecified, value. This is in contrast to a variable, which is not fixed.
a. Constant term0
b. Thing
c. Undefined
d. Undefined

18. Equivalence is the condition of being _____ or essentially equal.
a. Thing
b. Equivalent0
c. Undefined
d. Undefined

19. In mathematics, a _____ may be described informally as a number that can be given by an infinite decimal representation.
a. Thing
b. Real number0
c. Undefined
d. Undefined

20. The _____ of measurement are a globally standardized and modernized form of the metric system.

Chapter 4. Linear Inequalities and Systems of Linear Inequalities

    a. Units0
    c. Undefined
    b. Thing
    d. Undefined

21. A _____ is a set of possible values that a variable can take on in order to satisfy a given set of conditions, which may include equations and inequalities.
    a. Thing
    c. Undefined
    b. Solution set0
    d. Undefined

22. An _____ is a combination of numbers, operators, grouping symbols and/or free variables and bound variables arranged in a meaningful way which can be evaluated..
    a. Thing
    c. Undefined
    b. Expression0
    d. Undefined

23. _____, either of the curved-bracket punctuation marks that together make a set of _____
    a. Parentheses0
    c. Undefined
    b. Thing
    d. Undefined

24. In mathematics, and in particular in abstract algebra, the _____ is a property of binary operations that generalises the distributive law from elementary algebra.
    a. Thing
    c. Undefined
    b. Distributive property0
    d. Undefined

25. In mathematics, an inequality is a statement about the relative size or order of two objects. For example 14 > 10, or 14 is _____ 10.
    a. Greater than0
    c. Undefined
    b. Thing
    d. Undefined

26. _____ is the amount of time someone works beyond normal working hours.
    a. Compensatory time0
    c. Undefined
    b. Thing
    d. Undefined

27. Compass and straightedge or ruler-and-compass _____ is the _____ of lengths or angles using only an idealized ruler and compass.
    a. Thing
    c. Undefined
    b. Construction0
    d. Undefined

28. A _____ number is a positive integer which has a positive divisor other than one or itself.
    a. Thing
    c. Undefined
    b. Composite0
    d. Undefined

29. _____ is the calculated approximation of a result which is usable even if input data may be incomplete, uncertain, or noisy.
    a. Estimation0
    c. Undefined
    b. Concept
    d. Undefined

30. A _____ of a number is the product of that number with any integer.

a. Multiple0
b. Thing
c. Undefined
d. Undefined

31. Mathematical _____ are the wide variety of ways to capture an abstract mathematical concept or relationship.
a. Thing
b. Representations0
c. Undefined
d. Undefined

32. The plus and _____ signs are mathematical symbols used to represent the notions of positive and negative as well as the operations of addition and subtraction.
a. Minus0
b. Thing
c. Undefined
d. Undefined

33. _____ is the distance around a given two-dimensional object. As a general rule, the _____ of a polygon can always be calculated by adding all the length of the sides together. So, the formula for triangles is P = a + b + c, where a, b and c stand for each side of it. For quadrilaterals the equation is P = a + b + c + d. For equilateral polygons, P = na, where n is the number of sides and a is the side length.
a. Perimeter0
b. Thing
c. Undefined
d. Undefined

34. _____ is a business term for the amount of money that a company receives from its activities in a given period, mostly from sales of products and/or services to customers
a. Revenue0
b. Thing
c. Undefined
d. Undefined

35. Fixed costs are expenses whose total does not change in proportion to the activity of a business.Unit fixed costs decline with volume following a retangular hyperbola as the volume of production.Variable costs by contrast change in relation to the activity of a business such as sales or production volume.Along with variable costs,fixed costs make up one of the two components of total cost. In the most simple production function total cost is equal to fixed costs plus variable costs.In accounting terminology, fixed costs will broadly include all costs which are not included in cost of goods sold, and variable costs are those captured in costs of goods sold. The implicit assumption required to make the equivalence between the accounting and economics terminology is that the accounting period is equal to the period in which fixed costs do not vary in relation to production. In practice, this equivalence does not always hold and depending on the period under consideration by management, some overhead expenses can be adjusted by management, and the specific allocation of each expense to each category will be decided under cost accounting.In business planning and management accounting, usage of the terms fixed costs, variable costs and others will often differ from usage in economics, and may depend on the intended use. For example, costs may be segregated into per unit costs fixed costs per period, and variable costs as a proportion of revenue. Capital expenditures will usually be allocated separately, and depending on the purpose, a portion may be regularly allocated to expenses as depreciation and amortization and seen as a _____ per period, or the entire amount may be considered upfront fixed costs.
a. Thing
b. Fixed cost0
c. Undefined
d. Undefined

36. A _____ is one of the basic shapes of geometry: a polygon with three vertices and three sides which are straight line segments.

Chapter 4. Linear Inequalities and Systems of Linear Inequalities 51

   a. Thing
   c. Undefined
   b. Triangle0
   d. Undefined

37. A _____ is the result of the addition of a set of numbers. The numbers may be natural numbers, complex numbers, matrices, or still more complicated objects. An infinite _____ is a subtle procedure known as a series.
   a. Thing
   c. Undefined
   b. Sum0
   d. Undefined

38. In mathematics, _____ is an elementary arithmetic operation. When one of the numbers is a whole number, _____ is the repeated sum of the other number.
   a. Thing
   c. Undefined
   b. Multiplication0
   d. Undefined

39. In mathematics, a _____ is the result of multiplying, or an expression that identifies factors to be multiplied.
   a. Product0
   c. Undefined
   b. Thing
   d. Undefined

40. A _____ is a number that is less than zero.
   a. Negative number0
   c. Undefined
   b. Thing
   d. Undefined

41. _____ are the basic objects of study in graph theory. Informally speaking, a graph is a set of objects called points, nodes, or vertices connected by links called lines or edges.
   a. Thing
   c. Undefined
   b. Graphs0
   d. Undefined

42. Mathematical _____ really refers to two distinct areas of research: the first is the application of the techniques of formal _____ to mathematics and mathematical reasoning, and the second, in the other direction, the application of mathematical techniques to the representation and analysis of formal _____.
   a. Thing
   c. Undefined
   b. Logic0
   d. Undefined

43. In mathematics, a _____ is a constant multiplicative factor of a certain object. The object can be such things as a variable, a vector, a function, etc. For example, the _____ of $9x^2$ is 9.
   a. Coefficient0
   c. Undefined
   b. Thing
   d. Undefined

44. Two mathematical objects are equal if and only if they are precisely the same in every way. This defines a binary relation, _____, denoted by the sign of _____ "=" in such a way that the statement "x = y" means that x and y are equal.
   a. Equality0
   c. Undefined
   b. Thing
   d. Undefined

45. _____ interest refers to the fact that whenever interest is calculated, it is based not only on the original principal, but also on any unpaid interest that has been added to the principal.

Chapter 4. Linear Inequalities and Systems of Linear Inequalities

    a. Thing
    c. Undefined
    b. Compound0
    d. Undefined

46. _____ is a temperature scale named after the German physicist Daniel Gabriel _____ , who proposed it in 1724.
    a. Thing
    c. Undefined
    b. Fahrenheit0
    d. Undefined

47. _____ is a physical property of a system that underlies the common notions of hot and cold; something that is hotter has the greater _____.
    a. Thing
    c. Undefined
    b. Temperature0
    d. Undefined

48. _____ is, or relates to, the _____ temperature scale .
    a. Celsius0
    c. Undefined
    b. Thing
    d. Undefined

49. In set theory and other branches of mathematics, the _____ of a collection of sets is the set that contains everything that belongs to any of the sets, but nothing else.
    a. Union0
    c. Undefined
    b. Thing
    d. Undefined

50. _____ is a kind of property which exists as magnitude or multitude. It is among the basic classes of things along with quality, substance, change, and relation.
    a. Thing
    c. Undefined
    b. Amount0
    d. Undefined

51. _____ is the fee paid on borrowed money.
    a. Thing
    c. Undefined
    b. Interest0
    d. Undefined

52. A _____ is a unit of length, usually used to measure distance, in a number of different systems, including Imperial units, United States customary units and Norwegian/Swedish mil. Its size can vary from system to system, but in each is between 1 and 10 kilometers. In contemporary English contexts _____ refers to either:
    a. Thing
    c. Undefined
    b. Mile0
    d. Undefined

53. _____ is the application of tools and a processing medium to the transformation of raw materials into finished goods for sale.
    a. Thing
    c. Undefined
    b. Manufacturing0
    d. Undefined

54. In mathematics, _____ expressions is used to reduce the expression into the lowest possible term.
    a. Thing
    c. Undefined
    b. Simplifying0
    d. Undefined

Chapter 4. Linear Inequalities and Systems of Linear Inequalities 53

55. An _____ or member of a set is an object that when collected together make up the set.
   a. Element0
   b. Thing
   c. Undefined
   d. Undefined

56. In mathematics, the _____ , or members of a set or more generally a class are all those objects which when collected together make up the set or class.
   a. Elements0
   b. Thing
   c. Undefined
   d. Undefined

57. In mathematics and more specifically set theory, the _____ set is the unique set which contains no elements.
   a. Empty0
   b. Thing
   c. Undefined
   d. Undefined

58. A _____ is a one-dimensional picture in which the integers are shown as specially-marked points evenly spaced on a line.
   a. Number line0
   b. Thing
   c. Undefined
   d. Undefined

59. In mathematics, in the field of group theory, a _____ of a group is a quasisimple subnormal subgroup.
   a. Concept
   b. Component0
   c. Undefined
   d. Undefined

60. In mathematics, the _____ (or modulus) of a real number is its numerical value without regard to its sign.
   a. Absolute value0
   b. Thing
   c. Undefined
   d. Undefined

61. In mathematics, the _____ of a function is the set of all "output" values produced by that function. Given a function $f: A \to B$, the _____ of f, is defined to be the set $\{x \in B : x = f(a) \text{ for some } a \in A\}$.
   a. Range0
   b. Thing
   c. Undefined
   d. Undefined

62. In geometry, a _____ is defined as a quadrilateral where all four of its angles are right angles.
   a. Rectangle0
   b. Thing
   c. Undefined
   d. Undefined

63. The _____ integers are all the integers from zero on upwards.
   a. Thing
   b. Nonnegative0
   c. Undefined
   d. Undefined

64. _____ comes from the Latin word linearis, which means created by lines.
   a. Thing
   b. Linearity0
   c. Undefined
   d. Undefined

65. The _____ of a solid object is the three-dimensional concept of how much space it occupies, often quantified numerically.

Chapter 4. Linear Inequalities and Systems of Linear Inequalities

a. Thing
b. Volume0
c. Undefined
d. Undefined

66. _____ is the ability to hold, receive or absorb, or a measure thereof, similar to the concept of volume.
   a. Capacity0
   b. Concept
   c. Undefined
   d. Undefined

67. _____ is the difference of electrical potential between two points of an electrical or electronic circuit, expressed in volts
   a. Voltage0
   b. Thing
   c. Undefined
   d. Undefined

68. _____ is the study of error, particularly in the fields of applied mathematics, applied linguistics, statistics, and numerical analysis.
   a. Thing
   b. Error analysis0
   c. Undefined
   d. Undefined

69. _____ is a branch of mathematics concerning the study of structure, relation and quantity.
   a. Algebra0
   b. Concept
   c. Undefined
   d. Undefined

70. An _____ is a collection of two not necessarily distinct objects, one of which is distinguished as the first coordinate and the other as the second coordinate.
   a. Thing
   b. Ordered pair0
   c. Undefined
   d. Undefined

71. _____ is the scientific study of celestial objects such as stars, planets, comets, and galaxies; and phenomena that originate outside the Earth's atmosphere.
   a. Thing
   b. Astronomy0
   c. Undefined
   d. Undefined

72. In mathematics, a _____ is a two-dimensional manifold or surface that is perfectly flat.
   a. Thing
   b. Plane0
   c. Undefined
   d. Undefined

73. A _____ is a set of numbers that designate location in a given reference system, such as x,y in a planar _____ system or an x,y,z in a three-dimensional _____ system.
   a. Thing
   b. Coordinate0
   c. Undefined
   d. Undefined

74. In mathematics, the conjugate _____ or adjoint matrix of an m-by-n matrix A with complex entries is the n-by-m matrix A* obtained from A by taking the transpose and then taking the complex conjugate of each entry.
   a. Thing
   b. Pairs0
   c. Undefined
   d. Undefined

Chapter 4. Linear Inequalities and Systems of Linear Inequalities

75. Acid _____ ratio measures the ability of a company to use its near cash or quick assets to immediately extinguish its current liabilities.
    a. Test0
    b. Thing
    c. Undefined
    d. Undefined

76. In mathematics, the _____ of a coordinate system is the point where the axes of the system intersect.
    a. Origin0
    b. Thing
    c. Undefined
    d. Undefined

77. Any point where a graph makes contact with an coordinate axis is called an _____ of the graph
    a. Thing
    b. Intercept0
    c. Undefined
    d. Undefined

78. In mathematics, _____ geometry was the traditional name for the geometry of three-dimensional Euclidean space — for practical purposes the kind of space we live in.
    a. Solid0
    b. Thing
    c. Undefined
    d. Undefined

79. _____ over a given field is a polynomial with coefficients in that field.
    a. Algebraic equation0
    b. Thing
    c. Undefined
    d. Undefined

80. _____, from Latin meaning "to make progress", is defined in two different ways. Pure economic _____ is the increase in wealth that an investor has from making an investment, taking into consideration all costs associated with that investment including the opportunity cost of capital.
    a. Profit0
    b. Thing
    c. Undefined
    d. Undefined

81. In banking and accountancy, the outstanding _____ is the amount of money owned, or due, that remains in a deposit account or a loan account at a given date, after all past remittances, payments and withdrawal have been accounted for.
    a. Thing
    b. Balance0
    c. Undefined
    d. Undefined

82. In logic, Modus tollens (or Modus ponendo tollens) means to affirm by denying. It is the formal name for _____ proof or proof by contrapositive (contrapositive inference), often abbreviated to MT.
    a. Thing
    b. Indirect0
    c. Undefined
    d. Undefined

83. A _____ are accounts maintained by commercial banks, savings and loan associations, credit unions, and mutual savings banks that pay interest but can not be used directly as money by, for example, writing a cheque.
    a. Thing
    b. Savings account0
    c. Undefined
    d. Undefined

Chapter 5. Exponents and Operations with Polynomials

1. In mathematics, a _____ is the result of multiplying, or an expression that identifies factors to be multiplied.
   a. Thing
   b. Product0
   c. Undefined
   d. Undefined

2. Mathematical _____ is used to represent ideas.
   a. Notation0
   b. Thing
   c. Undefined
   d. Undefined

3. _____ is a notation for writing numbers that is often used by scientists and mathematicians to make it easier to write large and small numbers.
   a. Scientific notation0
   b. Thing
   c. Undefined
   d. Undefined

4. An _____ is a combination of numbers, operators, grouping symbols and/or free variables and bound variables arranged in a meaningful way which can be evaluated..
   a. Thing
   b. Expression0
   c. Undefined
   d. Undefined

5. _____ is a branch of mathematics concerning the study of structure, relation and quantity.
   a. Algebra0
   b. Concept
   c. Undefined
   d. Undefined

6. In mathematics, a _____ is an expression that is constructed from one or more variables and constants, using only the operations of addition, subtraction, multiplication, and constant positive whole number exponents. is a _____. Note in particular that division by an expression containing a variable is not in general allowed in polynomials. [1]
   a. Polynomial0
   b. Thing
   c. Undefined
   d. Undefined

7. The _____ governs the differentiation of products of differentiable functions.
   a. Thing
   b. Product rule0
   c. Undefined
   d. Undefined

8. _____ is a mathematical operation, written a^n, involving two numbers, the base a and the exponent n.
   a. Thing
   b. Exponentiating0
   c. Undefined
   d. Undefined

9. _____ is a mathematical operation, written a^n, involving two numbers, the base a and the exponent n.
   a. Exponentiation0
   b. Thing
   c. Undefined
   d. Undefined

10. _____ has many meanings, most of which simply .
    a. Power0
    b. Thing
    c. Undefined
    d. Undefined

11. _____ is a method for differentiating expressions involving exponentiation the power operation.

Chapter 5. Exponents and Operations with Polynomials

a. Power rule
b. Thing
c. Undefined
d. Undefined

12. A _____ is a special kind of ratio, indicating a relationship between two measurements with different units, such as miles to gallons or cents to pounds.
    a. Rate
    b. Thing
    c. Undefined
    d. Undefined

13. In business, particularly accounting, a _____ is the time intervals that the accounts, statement, payments, or other calculations cover.
    a. Thing
    b. Period
    c. Undefined
    d. Undefined

14. The _____ of an algebraic expression is the same equation, but without parentheses.
    a. Expanded form
    b. Thing
    c. Undefined
    d. Undefined

15. In mathematics, _____ growth occurs when the growth rate of a function is always proportional to the function's current size.
    a. Exponential
    b. Thing
    c. Undefined
    d. Undefined

16. A _____ is a symbolic representation denoting a quantity or expression. It often represents an "unknown" quantity that has the potential to change.
    a. Variable
    b. Thing
    c. Undefined
    d. Undefined

17. In abstract algebra, _____ consists of sets with binary operations that satisfy certain axioms.
    a. Grouping
    b. Thing
    c. Undefined
    d. Undefined

18. _____ are objects, characters, or other concrete representations of ideas, concepts, or other abstractions.
    a. Thing
    b. Symbols
    c. Undefined
    d. Undefined

19. In mathematics and the mathematical sciences, a _____ is a fixed, but possibly unspecified, value. This is in contrast to a variable, which is not fixed.
    a. Constant
    b. Thing
    c. Undefined
    d. Undefined

20. In mathematics, factorization (British English: factorisation) or factoring is the decomposition of an object (for example, a number, a polynomial, or a matrix) into a product of other objects, or _____, which when multiplied together give the original.
    a. Factors
    b. Thing
    c. Undefined
    d. Undefined

Chapter 5. Exponents and Operations with Polynomials

21. In mathematics, a _____ can mean either an element of the set {1, 2, 3, ...} (i.e the positive integers or the counting numbers) or an element of the set {0, 1, 2, 3, ...} (i.e. the non-negative integers).
    a. Natural number0
    b. Thing
    c. Undefined
    d. Undefined

22. In mathematics, a _____ may be described informally as a number that can be given by an infinite decimal representation.
    a. Real number0
    b. Thing
    c. Undefined
    d. Undefined

23. In mathematics, _____ is an elementary arithmetic operation. When one of the numbers is a whole number, _____ is the repeated sum of the other number.
    a. Thing
    b. Multiplication0
    c. Undefined
    d. Undefined

24. The _____ is a property of multiplication or addition where the product or sum remains the same, regardless of whether or not the order of the addends or factors are changed.
    a. Thing
    b. Commutative property0
    c. Undefined
    d. Undefined

25. In mathematics, a _____ is the end result of a division problem. It can also be expressed as the number of times the divisor divides into the dividend.
    a. Thing
    b. Quotient0
    c. Undefined
    d. Undefined

26. An _____ of a product of sums expresses it as a sum of products by using the fact that multiplication distributes over addition.
    a. Thing
    b. Expansion0
    c. Undefined
    d. Undefined

27. A _____ is a numeral used to indicate a count. The most common use of the word today is to name the part of a fraction that tells the number or count of equal parts.
    a. Thing
    b. Numerator0
    c. Undefined
    d. Undefined

28. A _____ is the part of a fraction that tells how many equal parts make up a whole, and which is used in the name of the fraction: "halves", "thirds", "fourths" or "quarters", "fifths" and so on.
    a. Concept
    b. Denominator0
    c. Undefined
    d. Undefined

29. In mathematics, _____ expressions is used to reduce the expression into the lowest possible term.
    a. Simplifying0
    b. Thing
    c. Undefined
    d. Undefined

30. In arithmetic and algebra, when a number or expression is both preceded and followed by a binary operation, an _____ is required for which operation should be applied first.

Chapter 5. Exponents and Operations with Polynomials

    a. Order of operations0
    c. Undefined
    b. Thing
    d. Undefined

31. In mathematics, and in particular in abstract algebra, the _____ is a property of binary operations that generalises the distributive law from elementary algebra.
    a. Thing
    c. Undefined
    b. Distributive property0
    d. Undefined

32. A _____ is the result of the addition of a set of numbers. The numbers may be natural numbers, complex numbers, matrices, or still more complicated objects. An infinite _____ is a subtle procedure known as a series.
    a. Thing
    c. Undefined
    b. Sum0
    d. Undefined

33. A _____ of a number is the product of that number with any integer.
    a. Multiple0
    c. Undefined
    b. Thing
    d. Undefined

34. Mathematical _____ are the wide variety of ways to capture an abstract mathematical concept or relationship.
    a. Thing
    c. Undefined
    b. Representations0
    d. Undefined

35. _____ is the fee paid on borrowed money.
    a. Interest0
    c. Undefined
    b. Thing
    d. Undefined

36. _____ interest refers to the fact that whenever interest is calculated, it is based not only on the original principal, but also on any unpaid interest that has been added to the principal.
    a. Compound0
    c. Undefined
    b. Thing
    d. Undefined

37. _____ refers to the fact that whenever interest is calculated, it is based not only on the original principal, but also on any unpaid interest that has been added to the principal. The more frequently interest is compounded, the faster the balance grows.
    a. Compound interest0
    c. Undefined
    b. Concept
    d. Undefined

38. An _____ is the fee paid on borrow money.
    a. Interest rate0
    c. Undefined
    b. Concept
    d. Undefined

39. A _____ is a three-dimensional solid object bounded by six square faces, facets, or sides, with three meeting at each vertex.
    a. Thing
    c. Undefined
    b. Cube0
    d. Undefined

40. _____ is a term applied when talking about the movement of air from one place to the next.

Chapter 5. Exponents and Operations with Polynomials

    a. Wind speed0   b. Thing
    c. Undefined   d. Undefined

41. In mathematics, an _____, mean, or central tendency of a data set refers to a measure of the "middle" or "expected" value of the data set.
    a. Concept   b. Average0
    c. Undefined   d. Undefined

42. The _____ is a method of finding the derivative of a function that is the quotient of two other functions for which derivatives exist.
    a. Thing   b. Quotient rule0
    c. Undefined   d. Undefined

43. In sociology and biology a _____ is the collection of people or organisms of a particular species living in a given geographic area or space, usually measured by a census.
    a. Population0   b. Thing
    c. Undefined   d. Undefined

44. Mathematical _____ really refers to two distinct areas of research: the first is the application of the techniques of formal _____ to mathematics and mathematical reasoning, and the second, in the other direction, the application of mathematical techniques to the representation and analysis of formal _____.
    a. Thing   b. Logic0
    c. Undefined   d. Undefined

45. In plane geometry, a _____ is a polygon with four equal sides, four right angles, and parallel opposite sides. In algebra, the _____ of a number is that number multiplied by itself.
    a. Thing   b. Square0
    c. Undefined   d. Undefined

46. _____ is the largest positive integer that divides both numbers without remainder.
    a. Common Factor0   b. Thing
    c. Undefined   d. Undefined

47. In mathematics, defined and _____ are used to explain whether or not expressions have meaningful, sensible, and unambiguous values.
    a. Thing   b. Undefined0
    c. Undefined   d. Undefined

48. The _____ of a function is an extension of the concept of a sum, and are identified or found through the use of integration.
    a. Integral0   b. Thing
    c. Undefined   d. Undefined

49. In mathematics, a _____ is an ordered list of objects. Like a set, it contains members, also called elements or terms, and the number of terms is called the length of the _____. Unlike a set, order matters, and the exact same elements can appear multiple times at different positions in the _____.

Chapter 5. Exponents and Operations with Polynomials

    a. Sequence0
    b. Thing
    c. Undefined
    d. Undefined

50. In mathematics, a _____ can mean either an element of the set {1, 2, 3, ...} (i.e the positive integers) or an element of the set {0, 1, 2, 3, ...} (i.e. the non-negative integers).
    a. Concept
    b. Whole number0
    c. Undefined
    d. Undefined

51. A _____ is a deliberate process for transforming one or more inputs into one or more results.
    a. Calculation0
    b. Thing
    c. Undefined
    d. Undefined

52. A _____ is a negotiable instrument instructing a financial institution to pay a specific amount of a specific currency from a specific demand account held in the maker/depositor's name with that institution. Both the maker and payee may be natural persons or legal entities.
    a. Check0
    b. Thing
    c. Undefined
    d. Undefined

53. The decimal separator is a symbol used to mark the boundary between the integral and the fractional parts of a decimal numeral. Terms implying the symbol used are _____ and decimal comma.
    a. Concept
    b. Decimal point0
    c. Undefined
    d. Undefined

54. _____ is the calculated approximation of a result which is usable even if input data may be incomplete, uncertain, or noisy.
    a. Concept
    b. Estimation0
    c. Undefined
    d. Undefined

55. In the mathematical field of numerical analysis, the _____ in some data is the discrepancy between an exact value and some approximation to it.
    a. Thing
    b. Approximation Error0
    c. Undefined
    d. Undefined

56. The act of _____ is the calculated approximation of a result which is usable even if input data may be incomplete, uncertain, or noisy.
    a. Thing
    b. Estimating0
    c. Undefined
    d. Undefined

57. Initial objects are also called _____, and terminal objects are also called final.
    a. Thing
    b. Coterminal0
    c. Undefined
    d. Undefined

58. _____ or investing is a term with several closely-related meanings in business management, finance and economics, related to saving or deferring consumption.

Chapter 5. Exponents and Operations with Polynomials

a. Investment0
b. Thing
c. Undefined
d. Undefined

59. _____ is a kind of property which exists as magnitude or multitude. It is among the basic classes of things along with quality, substance, change, and relation.
    a. Thing
    b. Amount0
    c. Undefined
    d. Undefined

60. John Brehaut _____ was born in Ashford, Kent, the third of five children.
    a. Wallis0
    b. Person
    c. Undefined
    d. Undefined

61. In mathematics, a _____ is a constant multiplicative factor of a certain object. The object can be such things as a variable, a vector, a function, etc. For example, the _____ of $9x^2$ is 9.
    a. Coefficient0
    b. Thing
    c. Undefined
    d. Undefined

62. _____, either of the curved-bracket punctuation marks that together make a set of _____
    a. Thing
    b. Parentheses0
    c. Undefined
    d. Undefined

63. A _____ is an instrument used in geometry technical drawing and engineering/building to measure distances and/or to rule straight lines.
    a. Ruler0
    b. Thing
    c. Undefined
    d. Undefined

64. A _____ is a number that is less than zero.
    a. Thing
    b. Negative number0
    c. Undefined
    d. Undefined

65. In mathematics, the multiplicative inverse of a number x, denoted 1/x or x^{-1}, is the number which, when multiplied by x, yields 1. The multiplicative inverse of x is also called the _____ of x.
    a. Reciprocal0
    b. Thing
    c. Undefined
    d. Undefined

66. _____ (or proportionality) are two quantities that vary in such a way that one of the quatities is a constant multiple of the other, or equivalently if they have a constant ratio.
    a. Thing
    b. Proportions0
    c. Undefined
    d. Undefined

67. The _____ of a mathematical object is its size: a property by which it can be larger or smaller than other objects of the same kind; in technical terms, an ordering of the class of objects to which it belongs.
    a. Magnitude0
    b. Thing
    c. Undefined
    d. Undefined

Chapter 5. Exponents and Operations with Polynomials

68. _____ is the mathematical action of repeatedly adding or subtracting one, usually to find out how many objects there are or to set aside a desired number of objects.
    a. Thing
    b. Counting0
    c. Undefined
    d. Undefined

69. In mathematics, an inequality is a statement about the relative size or order of two objects. For example 14 > 10, or 14 is _____ 10.
    a. Greater than0
    b. Thing
    c. Undefined
    d. Undefined

70. _____ is the writing of numbers in the base-ten numeral system, which uses various symbols called digits for ten distinct values 0, 1, 2, 3, 4, 5, 6, 7, 8 and 9 to represent numbers
    a. Decimal notation0
    b. Thing
    c. Undefined
    d. Undefined

71. In statistics, _____ means the most frequent value assumed by a random variable, or occurring in a sampling of a random variable.
    a. Concept
    b. Mode0
    c. Undefined
    d. Undefined

72. _____ is the estimation of a physical quantity such as distance, energy, temperature, or time.
    a. Thing
    b. Measurement0
    c. Undefined
    d. Undefined

73. The metre (or _____, see spelling differences) is a measure of length. It is the basic unit of length in the metric system and in the International System of Units (SI), used around the world for general and scientific purposes.
    a. Concept
    b. Meter0
    c. Undefined
    d. Undefined

74. The _____ of measurement are a globally standardized and modernized form of the metric system.
    a. Units0
    b. Thing
    c. Undefined
    d. Undefined

75. In common philosophical language, a proposition or _____, is the content of an assertion, that is, it is true-or-false and defined by the meaning of a particular piece of language.
    a. Statement0
    b. Concept
    c. Undefined
    d. Undefined

76. The _____, the average in everyday English, which is also called the arithmetic _____ (and is distinguished from the geometric _____ or harmonic _____). The average is also called the sample _____. The expected value of a random variable, which is also called the population _____.
    a. Thing
    b. Mean0
    c. Undefined
    d. Undefined

Chapter 5. Exponents and Operations with Polynomials

77. A _____, as defined by the International Astronomical Union, is a celestial body orbiting a star or stellar remnant that is massive enough to be rounded by its own gravity, not massive enough to cause thermonuclear fusion in its core, and has cleared its neighboring region of planetesimals.
   a. Planet0
   b. Thing
   c. Undefined
   d. Undefined

78. _____ is electromagnetic radiation with a wavelength that is visible to the eye (visible _____) or, in a technical or scientific context, electromagnetic radiation of any wavelength.
   a. Light0
   b. Thing
   c. Undefined
   d. Undefined

79. The _____ in a vacuum is an important physical constant denoted by the letter c for constant or the Latin word celeritas meaning "swiftness
   a. Thing
   b. Speed of light0
   c. Undefined
   d. Undefined

80. _____ is a physical property of a system that underlies the common notions of hot and cold; something that is hotter has the greater _____.
   a. Thing
   b. Temperature0
   c. Undefined
   d. Undefined

81. A _____ is a movement of an object in a circular motion. A two-dimensional object rotates around a center (or point) of _____. A three-dimensional object rotates around a line called an axis. If the axis of _____ is within the body, the body is said to rotate upon itself, or spin—which implies relative speed and perhaps free-movement with angular momentum. A circular motion about an external point, e.g. the Earth about the Sun, is called an orbit or more properly an orbital revolution.
   a. Rotation0
   b. Thing
   c. Undefined
   d. Undefined

82. _____ are the cyclic rizing and falling of Earth's ocean surface caused by the tidal forces of the Moon and the sun acting on the oceans.
   a. Thing
   b. Tides0
   c. Undefined
   d. Undefined

83. _____ is the force that opposes the relative motion or tendency toward such motion of two surfaces in contact.
   a. Friction0
   b. Thing
   c. Undefined
   d. Undefined

84. _____ is the transport of people on a trip/journey or the process or time involved in a person or object moving from one location to another.
   a. Thing
   b. Travel0
   c. Undefined
   d. Undefined

85. A _____ is a unit of length in the metric system, equal to one thousand metres, the current SI base unit of length

Chapter 5. Exponents and Operations with Polynomials

    a. Kilometer0
    b. Thing
    c. Undefined
    d. Undefined

86. A _____ is a statement or claimt that a particular event will occur in the future in more certain terms than a forecast.
    a. Thing
    b. Prediction0
    c. Undefined
    d. Undefined

87. The _____ . Utilizing a constellation of at least 24 medium Earth orbit satellites that transmit precise radio signals, the system enables a GPS receiver to determine its location, speed and direction..
    a. Thing
    b. Global positioning system0
    c. Undefined
    d. Undefined

88. _____ is the design, analysis, and/or construction of works for practical purposes.
    a. Engineering0
    b. Thing
    c. Undefined
    d. Undefined

89. _____ is the study of terms and their use — of words and compound words that are used in specific contexts.
    a. Thing
    b. Terminology0
    c. Undefined
    d. Undefined

90. In mathematics, a _____ is a particular kind of polynomial, having just one term.
    a. Thing
    b. Monomial0
    c. Undefined
    d. Undefined

91. The plus and _____ signs are mathematical symbols used to represent the notions of positive and negative as well as the operations of addition and subtraction.
    a. Thing
    b. Minus0
    c. Undefined
    d. Undefined

92. _____ is a fixed, but possibly unspecified, value. This is in contrast to a variable, which is not fixed.
    a. Constant term0
    b. Thing
    c. Undefined
    d. Undefined

93. A _____ is a polynomial consisting of three terms; in other words, it is the sum of three monomials.
    a. Trinomial0
    b. Thing
    c. Undefined
    d. Undefined

94. In mathematics, there are several meanings of _____ depending on the subject.
    a. Thing
    b. Degree0
    c. Undefined
    d. Undefined

95. _____ the expected value of a random variable displays the average or central value of the variable. It is a summary value of the distribution of the variable.

a. Determining0
b. Thing
c. Undefined
d. Undefined

96. The _____ is the maximum of the degrees of all terms in the polynomial.
   a. Thing
   b. Degree of a polynomial0
   c. Undefined
   d. Undefined

97. The mathematical concept of a _____ expresses the intuitive idea of deterministic dependence between two quantities, one of which is viewed as primary and the other as secondary. A _____ then is a way to associate a unique output for each input of a specified type, for example, a real number or an element of a given set.
   a. Function0
   b. Thing
   c. Undefined
   d. Undefined

98. _____, from Latin meaning "to make progress", is defined in two different ways. Pure economic _____ is the increase in wealth that an investor has from making an investment, taking into consideration all costs associated with that investment including the opportunity cost of capital.
   a. Profit0
   b. Thing
   c. Undefined
   d. Undefined

99. A _____ is one of the basic shapes of geometry: a polygon with three vertices and three sides which are straight line segments.
   a. Triangle0
   b. Thing
   c. Undefined
   d. Undefined

100. _____ is the distance around a given two-dimensional object. As a general rule, the _____ of a polygon can always be calculated by adding all the length of the sides together. So, the formula for triangles is P = a + b + c, where a, b and c stand for each side of it. For quadrilaterals the equation is P = a + b + c + d. For equilateral polygons, P = na, where n is the number of sides and a is the side length.
   a. Thing
   b. Perimeter0
   c. Undefined
   d. Undefined

101. _____ is the study of error, particularly in the fields of applied mathematics, applied linguistics, statistics, and numerical analysis.
   a. Thing
   b. Error analysis0
   c. Undefined
   d. Undefined

102. In elementary algebra, a _____ is a polynomial with two terms: the sum of two monomials. It is the simplest kind of polynomial except for a monomial.
   a. Thing
   b. Binomial0
   c. Undefined
   d. Undefined

103. In geometry, a _____ is defined as a quadrilateral where all four of its angles are right angles.
   a. Rectangle0
   b. Thing
   c. Undefined
   d. Undefined

Chapter 5. Exponents and Operations with Polynomials

104. _____ is a business term for the amount of money that a company receives from its activities in a given period, mostly from sales of products and/or services to customers
   a. Revenue0
   b. Thing
   c. Undefined
   d. Undefined

105. In mathematics, _____ is a property that a binary operation can have. Within an expression containing two or more of the same associative operators in a row, the order of operations does not matter as long as the sequence of the operands is not changed.
   a. Thing
   b. Associativity0
   c. Undefined
   d. Undefined

106. _____ over a given field is a polynomial with coefficients in that field.
   a. Algebraic equation0
   b. Thing
   c. Undefined
   d. Undefined

107. Acid _____ ratio measures the ability of a company to use its near cash or quick assets to immediately extinguish its current liabilities.
   a. Thing
   b. Test0
   c. Undefined
   d. Undefined

108. In mathematics, the _____ divisor of two non-zero integers, is the largest positive integer that divides both numbers without remainder.
   a. Greatest common0
   b. Thing
   c. Undefined
   d. Undefined

109. In Math the greates common divisor sometimes known as the _____ of two non- zero integers.
   a. Greatest common factor0
   b. Thing
   c. Undefined
   d. Undefined

110. In mathematics, _____ is the decomposition of an object into a product of other objects, or factors, which when multiplied together give the original.
   a. Factoring0
   b. Thing
   c. Undefined
   d. Undefined

111. In mathematics, a matrix can be thought of as each row or _____ being a vector. Hence, a space formed by row vectors or _____ vectors are said to be a row space or a _____ space.
   a. Concept
   b. Column0
   c. Undefined
   d. Undefined

112. In mathematics, the concept of a _____ tries to capture the intuitive idea of a geometrical one-dimensional and continuous object. A simple example is the circle.
   a. Curve0
   b. Thing
   c. Undefined
   d. Undefined

113. In mathematics, in the field of group theory, a _____ of a group is a quasisimple subnormal subgroup.

Chapter 5. Exponents and Operations with Polynomials

a. Concept
b. Component0
c. Undefined
d. Undefined

114. In mathematics, a _____ is a mathematical statement which appears likely to be true, but has not been formally proven to be true under the rules of mathematical logic.
a. Concept
b. Conjecture0
c. Undefined
d. Undefined

115. In abstract algebra, a _____ is an algebraic structure, a collection of elements and operations on them obeying defining axioms, that captures essential properties of both set operations and logic operations. Specifically, it deals with the set operations of intersection, union, complement; and the logic operations of AND, OR, NOT.
a. Thing
b. Boolean algebra0
c. Undefined
d. Undefined

116. In mathematics, a _____ of an integer n, also called a factor of n, is an integer which evenly divides n without leaving a remainder.
a. Divisor0
b. Thing
c. Undefined
d. Undefined

117. In arithmetic, _____ is a procedure for calculating the division of one integer, called the dividend, by another integer called the divisor, to produce a result called the quotient.
a. Thing
b. Long division0
c. Undefined
d. Undefined

118. The _____ are the only integral domain whose positive elements are well-ordered, and in which order is preserved by addition. Like the natural numbers, the _____ form a countably infinite set. The set of all _____ is usually denoted in mathematics by a boldface Z .
a. Integers0
b. Thing
c. Undefined
d. Undefined

119. _____ is a payment made by a company to its shareholders
a. Thing
b. Dividend0
c. Undefined
d. Undefined

120. A _____ is the part of the dividend that is left over when the dividend is not evenly divisible by the divisor.
a. Thing
b. Remainder0
c. Undefined
d. Undefined

121. Deductive _____ is the kind of _____ in which the conclusion is necessitated by, or reached from, previously known facts (the premises).
a. Thing
b. Reasoning0
c. Undefined
d. Undefined

122. _____ are the basic objects of study in graph theory. Informally speaking, a graph is a set of objects called points, nodes, or vertices connected by links called lines or edges.

Chapter 5. Exponents and Operations with Polynomials

a. Graphs0
b. Thing
c. Undefined
d. Undefined

123. In computer science an _____ is a data structure that consists of a group of elements having a single name that are accessed by indexing. In most programming languages each element has the same data type and the _____ occupies a continuous area of storage.
a. Thing
b. Array0
c. Undefined
d. Undefined

124. The term _____ can refer to an integer which is the square of some other integer, or an algebraic expression that can be factored as the square of some other expression.
a. Perfect square0
b. Thing
c. Undefined
d. Undefined

125. In mathematical logic, a Gödel numbering (or Gödel _____) is a function that assigns to each symbol and well-formed formula of some formal language a unique natural number called its Gödel number.
a. Code0
b. Thing
c. Undefined
d. Undefined

126. In mathematics the _____ refers to the identity: $a^2 - b^2 = (a+b)(a-b)$
a. Difference of two squares0
b. Thing
c. Undefined
d. Undefined

127. _____ or arithmetics is the oldest and most elementary branch of mathematics, used by almost everyone, for tasks ranging from simple daily counting to advanced science and business calculations.
a. Arithmetic0
b. Thing
c. Undefined
d. Undefined

128. In geographic information systems, a _____ comprises an entity with a geographic location, typically determined by points, arcs, or polygons. Carriageways and cadastres exemplify _____ data.
a. Feature0
b. Thing
c. Undefined
d. Undefined

129. A _____ is a function that assigns a number to subsets of a given set.
a. Thing
b. Measure0
c. Undefined
d. Undefined

130. The _____ of a solid object is the three-dimensional concept of how much space it occupies, often quantified numerically.
a. Thing
b. Volume0
c. Undefined
d. Undefined

131. In mathematics, a _____ is a quadric surface, with the following equation in Cartesian coordinates: $(x/_a)^2 + (y/_b)^2 = 1$.

Chapter 5. Exponents and Operations with Polynomials

a. Cylinder0
b. Thing
c. Undefined
d. Undefined

132. A _____ is an abstract model that uses mathematical language to describe the behavior of a system. Eykhoff defined a _____ as 'a representation of the essential aspects of an existing system which presents knowledge of that system in usable form'.
  a. Mathematical model0
  b. Thing
  c. Undefined
  d. Undefined

133. A _____ is a set whose members are members of another set or a set contained within another set.
  a. Thing
  b. Subset0
  c. Undefined
  d. Undefined

134. _____ are groups whose members are members of another set or a set contained within another set.
  a. Subsets0
  b. Thing
  c. Undefined
  d. Undefined

135. _____ is a sequence of numbers such that the difference of any two successive members of the sequence is a constant.
  a. Thing
  b. Arithmetic sequence0
  c. Undefined
  d. Undefined

136. An _____ is a collection of two not necessarily distinct objects, one of which is distinguished as the first coordinate and the other as the second coordinate.
  a. Ordered pair0
  b. Thing
  c. Undefined
  d. Undefined

137. The word _____ comes from the Latin word linearis, which means created by lines.
  a. Thing
  b. Linear0
  c. Undefined
  d. Undefined

138. A _____ is an equation in which each term is either a constant or the product of a constant times the first power of a variable.
  a. Thing
  b. Linear equation0
  c. Undefined
  d. Undefined

139. In mathematics, the _____ of two sets A and B is the set that contains all elements of A that also belong to B (or equivalently, all elements of B that also belong to A), but no other elements.
  a. Thing
  b. Intersection0
  c. Undefined
  d. Undefined

140. In astronomy, geography, geometry and related sciences and contexts, a plane is said to be _____ at a given point if it is locally perpendicular to the gradient of the gravity field, i.e., with the direction of the gravitational force at that point.
  a. Horizontal0
  b. Thing
  c. Undefined
  d. Undefined

Chapter 5. Exponents and Operations with Polynomials

141. A pair of angles are _____ if the sum of their angles is 90°.
    a. Complementary0
    b. Concept
    c. Undefined
    d. Undefined

142. In mathematics and logic, a _____ proof is a way of showing the truth or falsehood of a given statement by a straightforward combination of established facts, usually existing lemmas and theorems, without making any further assumptions.
    a. Direct0
    b. Thing
    c. Undefined
    d. Undefined

143. _____ is the relationship between two variables, like a ratio in which the two quantities being compared are different units.
    a. Thing
    b. Direct variation0
    c. Undefined
    d. Undefined

144. In mathematics, a _____ is a two-dimensional manifold or surface that is perfectly flat.
    a. Plane0
    b. Thing
    c. Undefined
    d. Undefined

145. _____ are a measure of time.
    a. Thing
    b. Minutes0
    c. Undefined
    d. Undefined

146. In chemistry, a _____ is substance made by combining two or more different materials in such a way that no chemical reaction occurs.
    a. Thing
    b. Mixture0
    c. Undefined
    d. Undefined

147. In mathematics, an _____ is a statement about the relative size or order of two objects.
    a. Thing
    b. Inequality0
    c. Undefined
    d. Undefined

148. A frame of _____ is a particular perspective from which the universe is observed.
    a. Reference0
    b. Thing
    c. Undefined
    d. Undefined

149. A _____ are accounts maintained by commercial banks, savings and loan associations, credit unions, and mutual savings banks that pay interest but can not be used directly as money by, for example, writing a cheque.
    a. Thing
    b. Savings account0
    c. Undefined
    d. Undefined

Chapter 6. Using Common Algebraic Functions

1. The mathematical concept of a _____ expresses the intuitive idea of deterministic dependence between two quantities, one of which is viewed as primary and the other as secondary. A _____ then is a way to associate a unique output for each input of a specified type, for example, a real number or an element of a given set.
   a. Thing
   b. Function0
   c. Undefined
   d. Undefined

2. Mathematical _____ are the wide variety of ways to capture an abstract mathematical concept or relationship.
   a. Representations0
   b. Thing
   c. Undefined
   d. Undefined

3. In mathematics, the _____ of a function is the set of all "output" values produced by that function. Given a function $f : A \to B$, the _____ of f, is defined to be the set $\{x \in B : x = f(a) \text{ for some } a \in A\}$.
   a. Thing
   b. Range0
   c. Undefined
   d. Undefined

4. In mathematics, a _____ of a k-place relation $L \subseteq X_1 \times \ldots \times X_k$ is one of the sets X_j, $1 \leq j \leq k$. In the special case where k = 2 and $L \subseteq X_1 \times X_2$ is a function $L : X_1 \to X_2$, it is conventional to refer to X_1 as the _____ of the function and to refer to X_2 as the codomain of the function.
   a. Domain0
   b. Thing
   c. Undefined
   d. Undefined

5. Mathematical _____ is used to represent ideas.
   a. Thing
   b. Notation0
   c. Undefined
   d. Undefined

6. The word _____ comes from the Latin word linearis, which means created by lines.
   a. Linear0
   b. Thing
   c. Undefined
   d. Undefined

7. A _____ is a first degree polynomial mathematical function of the form: f(x) = mx + b where m and b are real constants and x is a real variable.
   a. Linear function0
   b. Thing
   c. Undefined
   d. Undefined

8. _____ was a German mathematician and philosopher. He invented calculus independently of Newton, and his notation is the one in general use since.
   a. Person
   b. Leibniz0
   c. Undefined
   d. Undefined

9. Sir Isaac _____, was an English physicist, mathematician, astronomer, natural philosopher, and alchemist, regarded by many as the greatest figure in the history of science
   a. Newton0
   b. Person
   c. Undefined
   d. Undefined

10. _____ is a mathematical subject that includes the study of limits, derivatives, integrals, and power series and constitutes a major part of modern university curriculum.

Chapter 6. Using Common Algebraic Functions

    a. Calculus0
    c. Undefined
    b. Thing
    d. Undefined

11.   Sir _____ was an English physicist, mathematician, astronomer, natural philosopher, and alchemist, regarded by many as the greatest figure in the history of science.
    a. Person
    c. Undefined
    b. Isaac Newton0
    d. Undefined

12.   A _____ is a symbolic representation denoting a quantity or expression. It often represents an "unknown" quantity that has the potential to change.
    a. Variable0
    c. Undefined
    b. Thing
    d. Undefined

13.   _____ is the study of terms and their use — of words and compound words that are used in specific contexts.
    a. Thing
    c. Undefined
    b. Terminology0
    d. Undefined

14.   _____ is a branch of mathematics concerning the study of structure, relation and quantity.
    a. Algebra0
    c. Undefined
    b. Concept
    d. Undefined

15.   An _____ or member of a set is an object that when collected together make up the set.
    a. Thing
    c. Undefined
    b. Element0
    d. Undefined

16.   In mathematics, the conjugate _____ or adjoint matrix of an m-by-n matrix A with complex entries is the n-by-m matrix A* obtained from A by taking the transpose and then taking the complex conjugate of each entry.
    a. Pairs0
    c. Undefined
    b. Thing
    d. Undefined

17.   In mathematics, the _____ , or members of a set or more generally a class are all those objects which when collected together make up the set or class.
    a. Thing
    c. Undefined
    b. Elements0
    d. Undefined

18.   The _____ of a solid object is the three-dimensional concept of how much space it occupies, often quantified numerically.
    a. Thing
    c. Undefined
    b. Volume0
    d. Undefined

19.   A _____ is a set of numbers that designate location in a given reference system, such as x,y in a planar _____ system or an x,y,z in a three-dimensional _____ system.
    a. Thing
    c. Undefined
    b. Coordinate0
    d. Undefined

20. An _____ is a collection of two not necessarily distinct objects, one of which is distinguished as the first coordinate and the other as the second coordinate.
   a. Thing
   b. Ordered pair0
   c. Undefined
   d. Undefined

21. _____, either of the curved-bracket punctuation marks that together make a set of _____
   a. Thing
   b. Parentheses0
   c. Undefined
   d. Undefined

22. In mathematics and its applications, a _____ is a system for assigning an n-tuple of numbers or scalars to each point in an n-dimensional space.
   a. Concept
   b. Coordinate system0
   c. Undefined
   d. Undefined

23. The _____, the average in everyday English, which is also called the arithmetic _____ (and is distinguished from the geometric _____ or harmonic _____). The average is also called the sample _____. The expected value of a random variable, which is also called the population _____.
   a. Mean0
   b. Thing
   c. Undefined
   d. Undefined

24. _____ means of or relating to the French philosopher and mathematician René Descartes.
   a. Thing
   b. Cartesian0
   c. Undefined
   d. Undefined

25. In mathematics, the _____ is used to determine each point uniquely in a plane through two numbers, usually called the x-coordinate and the y-coordinate of the point.
   a. Cartesian coordinate system0
   b. Thing
   c. Undefined
   d. Undefined

26. _____ are the basic objects of study in graph theory. Informally speaking, a graph is a set of objects called points, nodes, or vertices connected by links called lines or edges.
   a. Thing
   b. Graphs0
   c. Undefined
   d. Undefined

27. In mathematics, a _____ is a two-dimensional manifold or surface that is perfectly flat.
   a. Plane0
   b. Thing
   c. Undefined
   d. Undefined

28. In mathematics, an _____ is any of the arguments, i.e. "inputs", to a function. Thus if we have a function f(x), then x is a _____.
   a. Thing
   b. Independent variable0
   c. Undefined
   d. Undefined

29. In a function the _____, is the variable which is the value, i.e. the "output", of the function.

Chapter 6. Using Common Algebraic Functions

a. Dependent variable0
b. Thing
c. Undefined
d. Undefined

30. In mathematics, a _____ is any one of several different types of functions, mappings, operations, or transformations.
    a. Projection0
    b. Thing
    c. Undefined
    d. Undefined

31. In mathematics, the _____ f is the collection of all ordered pairs . In particular, graph means the graphical representation of this collection, in the form of a curve or surface, together with axes, etc. Graphing on a Cartesian plane is sometimes referred to as curve sketching.
    a. Graph of a function0
    b. Thing
    c. Undefined
    d. Undefined

32. _____ the expected value of a random variable displays the average or central value of the variable. It is a summary value of the distribution of the variable.
    a. Determining0
    b. Thing
    c. Undefined
    d. Undefined

33. In geometry, an _____ is a point at which a line segment or ray terminates.
    a. Thing
    b. Endpoint0
    c. Undefined
    d. Undefined

34. In mathematics, a _____ may be described informally as a number that can be given by an infinite decimal representation.
    a. Real number0
    b. Thing
    c. Undefined
    d. Undefined

35. _____ is a test to determine if a relation or its graph is a function or not
    a. Vertical line test0
    b. Thing
    c. Undefined
    d. Undefined

36. Acid _____ ratio measures the ability of a company to use its near cash or quick assets to immediately extinguish its current liabilities.
    a. Thing
    b. Test0
    c. Undefined
    d. Undefined

37. _____ is often used to describe the measurement of the steepness, incline, gradient, or grade of a straight line. The _____ is defined as the ratio of the "rise" divided by the "run" between two points on a line, or in other words, the ratio of the altitude change to the horizontal distance between any two points on the line.
    a. Slope0
    b. Thing
    c. Undefined
    d. Undefined

38. An _____ is a combination of numbers, operators, grouping symbols and/or free variables and bound variables arranged in a meaningful way which can be evaluated..

a. Thing
b. Expression0
c. Undefined
d. Undefined

39. In elementary algebra, an _____ is a set that contains every real number between two indicated numbers and may contain the two numbers themselves.
   a. Thing
   b. Interval0
   c. Undefined
   d. Undefined

40. A _____ of a number is the product of that number with any integer.
   a. Multiple0
   b. Thing
   c. Undefined
   d. Undefined

41. In statistics, a _____ is a graphical display of tabulated frequencies.
   a. Concept
   b. Histogram0
   c. Undefined
   d. Undefined

42. _____ is a physical property of a system that underlies the common notions of hot and cold; something that is hotter has the greater _____.
   a. Thing
   b. Temperature0
   c. Undefined
   d. Undefined

43. In mathematics and the mathematical sciences, a _____ is a fixed, but possibly unspecified, value. This is in contrast to a variable, which is not fixed.
   a. Thing
   b. Constant0
   c. Undefined
   d. Undefined

44. A _____ is the sum of the elements of a sequence.
   a. Thing
   b. Series0
   c. Undefined
   d. Undefined

45. In geometry, the _____ of an object is a point in some sense in the middle of the object.
   a. Thing
   b. Center0
   c. Undefined
   d. Undefined

46. _____, from Latin meaning "to make progress", is defined in two different ways. Pure economic _____ is the increase in wealth that an investor has from making an investment, taking into consideration all costs associated with that investment including the opportunity cost of capital.
   a. Profit0
   b. Thing
   c. Undefined
   d. Undefined

47. In mathematics, there are several meanings of _____ depending on the subject.
   a. Degree0
   b. Thing
   c. Undefined
   d. Undefined

48. A _____ is a quantity that denotes the proportional amount or magnitude of one quantity relative to another.

Chapter 6. Using Common Algebraic Functions

    a. Thing
    c. Undefined
    b. Ratio0
    d. Undefined

49. In mathematics, the _____ (or modulus) of a real number is its numerical value without regard to its sign.
    a. Absolute value0
    c. Undefined
    b. Thing
    d. Undefined

50. The _____ of measurement are a globally standardized and modernized form of the metric system.
    a. Units0
    c. Undefined
    b. Thing
    d. Undefined

51. A _____ is a number that is less than zero.
    a. Thing
    c. Undefined
    b. Negative number0
    d. Undefined

52. In mathematics, defined and _____ are used to explain whether or not expressions have meaningful, sensible, and unambiguous values.
    a. Undefined0
    c. Undefined
    b. Thing
    d. Undefined

53. In astronomy, geography, geometry and related sciences and contexts, a plane is said to be _____ at a given point if it is locally perpendicular to the gradient of the gravity field, i.e., with the direction of the gravitational force at that point.
    a. Thing
    c. Undefined
    b. Horizontal0
    d. Undefined

54. In mathematics, a _____ is a constant multiplicative factor of a certain object. The object can be such things as a variable, a vector, a function, etc. For example, the _____ of $9x^2$ is 9.
    a. Thing
    c. Undefined
    b. Coefficient0
    d. Undefined

55. A _____ is a negotiable instrument instructing a financial institution to pay a specific amount of a specific currency from a specific demand account held in the maker/depositor's name with that institution. Both the maker and payee may be natural persons or legal entities.
    a. Check0
    c. Undefined
    b. Thing
    d. Undefined

56. One of the three formats applicable to a quadratic function is the _____ which is defined as $f = ax^2 + bx + c$.
    a. General form0
    c. Undefined
    b. Thing
    d. Undefined

57. _____ is the transport of people on a trip/journey or the process or time involved in a person or object moving from one location to another.
    a. Thing
    c. Undefined
    b. Travel0
    d. Undefined

Chapter 6. Using Common Algebraic Functions

58. A _____ is an equation in which each term is either a constant or the product of a constant times the first power of a variable.
    a. Thing
    b. Linear equation0
    c. Undefined
    d. Undefined

59. The _____ of a geographic location is its height above a fixed reference point, often the mean sea level.
    a. Elevation0
    b. Thing
    c. Undefined
    d. Undefined

60. _____ has many meanings, most of which simply .
    a. Power0
    b. Thing
    c. Undefined
    d. Undefined

61. The existence and properties of _____ are the basis of Euclid's parallel postulate. _____ are two lines on the same plane that do not intersect even assuming that lines extend to infinity in either direction.
    a. Thing
    b. Parallel lines0
    c. Undefined
    d. Undefined

62. In mathematics, the multiplicative inverse of a number x, denoted $1/x$ or x^{-1}, is the number which, when multiplied by x, yields 1. The multiplicative inverse of x is also called the _____ of x.
    a. Reciprocal0
    b. Thing
    c. Undefined
    d. Undefined

63. In mathematics, the additive inverse, or _____ of a number n is the number that, when added to n, yields zero. The additive inverse of n is denoted −n. For example, 7 is −7, because 7 + (−7) = 0, and the additive inverse of −0.3 is 0.3, because −0.3 + 0.3 = 0.
    a. Opposite0
    b. Thing
    c. Undefined
    d. Undefined

64. In geometry, two lines or planes if one falls on the other in such a way as to create congruent adjacent angles. The term may be used as a noun or adjective. Thus, referring to Figure 1, the line AB is the _____ to CD through the point B.
    a. Perpendicular0
    b. Thing
    c. Undefined
    d. Undefined

65. In mathematics, the _____ of a number n is the number that, when added to n, yields zero. The _____ of n is denoted −n. For example, 7 is −7, because 7 + (−7) = 0, and the _____ of −0.3 is 0.3, because −0.3 + 0.3 = 0.
    a. Thing
    b. Additive inverse0
    c. Undefined
    d. Undefined

66. _____ over a given field is a polynomial with coefficients in that field.
    a. Algebraic equation0
    b. Thing
    c. Undefined
    d. Undefined

67. The _____ of a ring *R* is defined to be the smallest positive integer *n* such that *n* a = 0, for all a in R.

a. Characteristic0
b. Thing
c. Undefined
d. Undefined

68. In mathematics, the concept of a _____ tries to capture the intuitive idea of a geometrical one-dimensional and continuous object. A simple example is the circle.
   a. Curve0
   b. Thing
   c. Undefined
   d. Undefined

69. In geometry, a _____ is a special kind of point, usually a corner of a polygon, polyhedron, or higher dimensional polytope. In the geometry of curves a _____ is a point of where the first derivative of curvature is zero. In graph theory, a _____ is the fundamental unit out of which graphs are formed
   a. Vertex0
   b. Thing
   c. Undefined
   d. Undefined

70. _____ is the notation in which permitted values for a variable are expressed as ranging over a certain interval; "5 < x < 9" is an example of the application of _____.
   a. Thing
   b. Interval notation0
   c. Undefined
   d. Undefined

71. A _____ is a polynomial function of the form $f(x) = ax^2 + bx + c$, where a, b, c are real numbers and a , 0.
   a. Event
   b. Quadratic function0
   c. Undefined
   d. Undefined

72. In mathematics, the _____ is a conic section generated by the intersection of a right circular conical surface and a plane parallel to a generating straight line of that surface. It can also be defined as locus of points in a plane which are equidistant from a given point.
   a. Parabola0
   b. Thing
   c. Undefined
   d. Undefined

73. _____ are external two-dimensional outlines, with the appearance or configuration of some thing - in contrast to the matter or content or substance of which it is composed.
   a. Thing
   b. Shapes0
   c. Undefined
   d. Undefined

74. In geographic information systems, a _____ comprises an entity with a geographic location, typically determined by points, arcs, or polygons. Carriageways and cadastres exemplify _____ data.
   a. Thing
   b. Feature0
   c. Undefined
   d. Undefined

75. In plane geometry, a _____ is a polygon with four equal sides, four right angles, and parallel opposite sides. In algebra, the _____ of a number is that number multiplied by itself.
   a. Square0
   b. Thing
   c. Undefined
   d. Undefined

76. In mathematics, a _____ of a number x is a number r such that $r^2 = x$, or in words, a number r whose square (the result of multiplying the number by itself) is x.

Chapter 6. Using Common Algebraic Functions

    a. Thing
    b. Square root0
    c. Undefined
    d. Undefined

77. In mathematics, a _____ of a complex-valued function f is a member x of the domain of f such that f(x) vanishes at x, that is, x : f (x) = 0.
    a. Thing
    b. Root0
    c. Undefined
    d. Undefined

78. _____ is a function of the form
    a. Thing
    b. Cubic function0
    c. Undefined
    d. Undefined

79. A _____ is a three-dimensional solid object bounded by six square faces, facets, or sides, with three meeting at each vertex.
    a. Cube0
    b. Thing
    c. Undefined
    d. Undefined

80. A _____ of a number is a number a such that $a^3 = x$.
    a. Thing
    b. Cube root0
    c. Undefined
    d. Undefined

81. Any point where a graph makes contact with an coordinate axis is called an _____ of the graph
    a. Intercept0
    b. Thing
    c. Undefined
    d. Undefined

82. The _____ integers are all the integers from zero on upwards.
    a. Nonnegative0
    b. Thing
    c. Undefined
    d. Undefined

83. In mathematics, an _____ is a statement about the relative size or order of two objects.
    a. Thing
    b. Inequality0
    c. Undefined
    d. Undefined

84. In mathematics, an inequality is a statement about the relative size or order of two objects. For example 14 > 10, or 14 is _____ 10.
    a. Greater than0
    b. Thing
    c. Undefined
    d. Undefined

85. _____ is dedicated to the interests of mathematical research and scholarship, which it does with various publications and conferences as well as annual monetary awards to mathematicians.
    a. Thing
    b. American Mathematical Society0
    c. Undefined
    d. Undefined

86. A _____ is a one-dimensional picture in which the integers are shown as specially-marked points evenly spaced on a line.

Chapter 6. Using Common Algebraic Functions   81

    a. Thing
    b. Number line0
    c. Undefined
    d. Undefined

87. In Euclidean geometry, a _____ is moving every point a constant distance in a specified direction.
    a. Concept
    b. Translation0
    c. Undefined
    d. Undefined

88. _____ is a synonym for information.
    a. Data0
    b. Thing
    c. Undefined
    d. Undefined

89. Equivalence is the condition of being _____ or essentially equal.
    a. Equivalent0
    b. Thing
    c. Undefined
    d. Undefined

90. In mathematics, a _____ is an ordered list of objects. Like a set, it contains members, also called elements or terms, and the number of terms is called the length of the _____. Unlike a set, order matters, and the exact same elements can appear multiple times at different positions in the _____.
    a. Sequence0
    b. Thing
    c. Undefined
    d. Undefined

91. In Euclidean geometry, a uniform _____ is a linear transformation that enlargers or diminishes objects, and whose _____ factor is the same in all directions. This is also called homothethy.
    a. Thing
    b. Scale0
    c. Undefined
    d. Undefined

92. _____ is, or relates to, the _____ temperature scale .
    a. Thing
    b. Celsius0
    c. Undefined
    d. Undefined

93. A frame of _____ is a particular perspective from which the universe is observed.
    a. Reference0
    b. Thing
    c. Undefined
    d. Undefined

94. _____ is a business term for the amount of money that a company receives from its activities in a given period, mostly from sales of products and/or services to customers
    a. Revenue0
    b. Thing
    c. Undefined
    d. Undefined

95. In mathematics, a _____ (also spelled reflexion) is a map that transforms an object into its mirror image.
    a. Reflection0
    b. Concept
    c. Undefined
    d. Undefined

96. In mathematics, factorization (British English: factorisation) or factoring is the decomposition of an object (for example, a number, a polynomial, or a matrix) into a product of other objects, or _____, which when multiplied together give the original.

Chapter 6. Using Common Algebraic Functions

a. Factors0
b. Thing
c. Undefined
d. Undefined

97. In mathematics, _____ is a part of the set theoretic notion of function.
  a. Image0
  b. Thing
  c. Undefined
  d. Undefined

98. _____ element of an element x with respect to a binary operation * with identity element e is an element y such that x * y = y * x = e. In particular,
  a. Inverse0
  b. Thing
  c. Undefined
  d. Undefined

99. In mathematics, the _____ inverse, or opposite, of a number n is the number that, when added to n, yields zero. The _____ inverse of n is denoted −n.
  a. Thing
  b. Additive0
  c. Undefined
  d. Undefined

100. A _____ is a special kind of ratio, indicating a relationship between two measurements with different units, such as miles to gallons or cents to pounds.
  a. Thing
  b. Rate0
  c. Undefined
  d. Undefined

101. _____ is a kind of property which exists as magnitude or multitude. It is among the basic classes of things along with quality, substance, change, and relation.
  a. Thing
  b. Amount0
  c. Undefined
  d. Undefined

102. _____ is the fee paid on borrowed money.
  a. Thing
  b. Interest0
  c. Undefined
  d. Undefined

103. An _____ is the fee paid on borrow money.
  a. Concept
  b. Interest rate0
  c. Undefined
  d. Undefined

104. _____ or investing is a term with several closely-related meanings in business management, finance and economics, related to saving or deferring consumption.
  a. Thing
  b. Investment0
  c. Undefined
  d. Undefined

105. _____ is finding a curve which matches a series of data points and possibly other constraints.
  a. Curve fitting0
  b. Thing
  c. Undefined
  d. Undefined

106. A _____ is a simplified and structured visual representation of concepts, ideas, constructions, relations, statistical data, anatomy etc used in all aspects of human activities to visualize and clarify the topic.

Chapter 6. Using Common Algebraic Functions

   a. Thing
   c. Undefined
   b. Diagram0
   d. Undefined

107. _____ is a mathematical science pertaining to the collection, analysis, interpretation or explanation, and presentation of data. It is applicable to a wide variety of academic disciplines, from the physical and social sciences to the humanities.
   a. Thing
   c. Undefined
   b. Statistics0
   d. Undefined

108. In mathematics, _____ are the intuitive idea of a geometrical one-dimensional and continuous object.
   a. Curves0
   c. Undefined
   b. Thing
   d. Undefined

109. In mathematics, a _____ is a polynomial equation of the second degree. The general form is $ax^2 + bx + c = 0$.
   a. Thing
   c. Undefined
   b. Quadratic equation0
   d. Undefined

110. _____ is the property of a physical object that quantifies the amount of matter and energy it is equivalent to.
   a. Thing
   c. Undefined
   b. Mass0
   d. Undefined

111. In the scientific method, an _____ (Latin: ex-+-periri, "of (or from) trying"), is a set of actions and observations, performed in the context of solving a particular problem or question, in order to support or falsify a hypothesis or research concerning phenomena.
   a. Thing
   c. Undefined
   b. Experiment0
   d. Undefined

112. _____, Greek for "knowledge of nature," is the branch of science concerned with the discovery and characterization of universal laws which govern matter, energy, space, and time.
   a. Physics0
   c. Undefined
   b. Thing
   d. Undefined

113. In geometry, a line _____ is a part of a line that is bounded by two end points, and contains every point on the line between its end points.
   a. Segment0
   c. Undefined
   b. Conccpt
   d. Undefined

114. _____ comes from the Latin word linearis, which means created by lines.
   a. Thing
   c. Undefined
   b. Linearity0
   d. Undefined

115. In mathematics, a _____ is an expression that is constructed from one or more variables and constants, using only the operations of addition, subtraction, multiplication, and constant positive whole number exponents. is a _____. Note in particular that division by an expression containing a variable is not in general allowed in polynomials. [1]

Chapter 6. Using Common Algebraic Functions

    a. Polynomial0
    b. Thing
    c. Undefined
    d. Undefined

116. _____ is the largest positive integer that divides both numbers without remainder.
    a. Thing
    b. Common Factor0
    c. Undefined
    d. Undefined

117. In mathematics, _____ is the decomposition of an object into a product of other objects, or factors, which when multiplied together give the original.
    a. Factoring0
    b. Thing
    c. Undefined
    d. Undefined

118. In mathematics, the _____ divisor of two non-zero integers, is the largest positive integer that divides both numbers without remainder.
    a. Thing
    b. Greatest common0
    c. Undefined
    d. Undefined

119. In Math the greates common divisor sometimes known as the _____ of two non- zero integers.
    a. Thing
    b. Greatest common factor0
    c. Undefined
    d. Undefined

120. In elementary algebra, a _____ is a polynomial with two terms: the sum of two monomials. It is the simplest kind of polynomial except for a monomial.
    a. Binomial0
    b. Thing
    c. Undefined
    d. Undefined

121. In mathematics, and in particular in abstract algebra, the _____ is a property of binary operations that generalises the distributive law from elementary algebra.
    a. Thing
    b. Distributive property0
    c. Undefined
    d. Undefined

122. A _____ is a polynomial consisting of three terms; in other words, it is the sum of three monomials.
    a. Thing
    b. Trinomial0
    c. Undefined
    d. Undefined

123. In mathematics, a _____ is a number in the form of a + bi where a and b are real numbers, and i is the imaginary unit, with the property i 2 = −1. The real number a is called the real part of the _____, and the real number b is the imaginary part.
    a. Complex number0
    b. Thing
    c. Undefined
    d. Undefined

124. _____ is a regression method that models the relationship between a dependent variable Y, independent variables Xp, and a random term å.
    a. Thing
    b. Linear regression0
    c. Undefined
    d. Undefined

Chapter 6. Using Common Algebraic Functions

125. In mathematics, _____ is an elementary arithmetic operation. When one of the numbers is a whole number, _____ is the repeated sum of the other number.
 a. Multiplication0 b. Thing
 c. Undefined d. Undefined

126. _____ are a measure of time.
 a. Minutes0 b. Thing
 c. Undefined d. Undefined

127. Initial objects are also called _____, and terminal objects are also called final.
 a. Coterminal0 b. Thing
 c. Undefined d. Undefined

128. _____ is a notation for writing numbers that is often used by scientists and mathematicians to make it easier to write large and small numbers.
 a. Scientific notation0 b. Thing
 c. Undefined d. Undefined

Chapter 7. Another Look at Factoring Polynomials

1. In mathematics, a _____ is an expression that is constructed from one or more variables and constants, using only the operations of addition, subtraction, multiplication, and constant positive whole number exponents. is a _____. Note in particular that division by an expression containing a variable is not in general allowed in polynomials. [1]
    a. Thing
    b. Polynomial0
    c. Undefined
    d. Undefined

2. In mathematics, in the field of group theory, a _____ of a group is a quasisimple subnormal subgroup.
    a. Concept
    b. Component0
    c. Undefined
    d. Undefined

3. A _____ is a polynomial consisting of three terms; in other words, it is the sum of three monomials.
    a. Trinomial0
    b. Thing
    c. Undefined
    d. Undefined

4. In mathematics, _____ is the decomposition of an object into a product of other objects, or factors, which when multiplied together give the original.
    a. Thing
    b. Factoring0
    c. Undefined
    d. Undefined

5. _____ is a natural number that has exactly two distinct natural number divisors, which are 1 and the _____ itself.
    a. Thing
    b. Prime number0
    c. Undefined
    d. Undefined

6. _____ are the basic objects of study in graph theory. Informally speaking, a graph is a set of objects called points, nodes, or vertices connected by links called lines or edges.
    a. Thing
    b. Graphs0
    c. Undefined
    d. Undefined

7. In mathematics, a _____ number (or a _____) is a natural number that has exactly two (distinct) natural number divisors, which are 1 and the _____ number itself.
    a. Prime0
    b. Thing
    c. Undefined
    d. Undefined

8. In mathematics, factorization (British English: factorisation) or factoring is the decomposition of an object (for example, a number, a polynomial, or a matrix) into a product of other objects, or _____, which when multiplied together give the original.
    a. Factors0
    b. Thing
    c. Undefined
    d. Undefined

9. The _____ are the only integral domain whose positive elements are well-ordered, and in which order is preserved by addition. Like the natural numbers, the _____ form a countably infinite set. The set of all _____ is usually denoted in mathematics by a boldface Z .
    a. Integers0
    b. Thing
    c. Undefined
    d. Undefined

10. The word _____ comes from the Latin word linearis, which means created by lines.

a. Linear0   b. Thing
c. Undefined   d. Undefined

11. In mathematics and the mathematical sciences, a _____ is a fixed, but possibly unspecified, value. This is in contrast to a variable, which is not fixed.
    a. Thing
    b. Constant0
    c. Undefined
    d. Undefined

12. _____ is a fixed, but possibly unspecified, value. This is in contrast to a variable, which is not fixed.
    a. Constant term0
    b. Thing
    c. Undefined
    d. Undefined

13. In mathematics, the _____ divisor of two non-zero integers, is the largest positive integer that divides both numbers without remainder.
    a. Thing
    b. Greatest common0
    c. Undefined
    d. Undefined

14. In Math the greates common divisor sometimes known as the _____ of two non- zero integers.
    a. Greatest common factor0
    b. Thing
    c. Undefined
    d. Undefined

15. _____ is the largest positive integer that divides both numbers without remainder.
    a. Common Factor0
    b. Thing
    c. Undefined
    d. Undefined

16. A _____ is the result of the addition of a set of numbers. The numbers may be natural numbers, complex numbers, matrices, or still more complicated objects. An infinite _____ is a subtle procedure known as a series.
    a. Sum0
    b. Thing
    c. Undefined
    d. Undefined

17. In mathematics, a _____ is the result of multiplying, or an expression that identifies factors to be multiplied.
    a. Product0
    b. Thing
    c. Undefined
    d. Undefined

18. In mathematics, a _____ is a constant multiplicative factor of a certain object. The object can be such things as a variable, a vector, a function, etc. For example, the _____ of $9x^2$ is 9.
    a. Coefficient0
    b. Thing
    c. Undefined
    d. Undefined

19. In elementary algebra, a _____ is a polynomial with two terms: the sum of two monomials. It is the simplest kind of polynomial except for a monomial.
    a. Binomial0
    b. Thing
    c. Undefined
    d. Undefined

20. In mathematics, _____ is an elementary arithmetic operation. When one of the numbers is a whole number, _____ is the repeated sum of the other number.

Chapter 7. Another Look at Factoring Polynomials

a. Multiplication0
b. Thing
c. Undefined
d. Undefined

21. In mathematics, the conjugate _____ or adjoint matrix of an m-by-n matrix A with complex entries is the n-by-m matrix A* obtained from A by taking the transpose and then taking the complex conjugate of each entry.
a. Pairs0
b. Thing
c. Undefined
d. Undefined

22. In mathematics, and in particular in abstract algebra, the _____ is a property of binary operations that generalises the distributive law from elementary algebra.
a. Distributive property0
b. Thing
c. Undefined
d. Undefined

23. In abstract algebra, _____ consists of sets with binary operations that satisfy certain axioms.
a. Grouping0
b. Thing
c. Undefined
d. Undefined

24. In mathematics, the additive inverse, or _____ of a number n is the number that, when added to n, yields zero. The additive inverse of n is denoted −n. For example, 7 is −7, because 7 + (−7) = 0, and the additive inverse of −0.3 is 0.3, because −0.3 + 0.3 = 0.
a. Thing
b. Opposite0
c. Undefined
d. Undefined

25. In mathematics, the _____ of a number n is the number that, when added to n, yields zero. The _____ of n is denoted −n. For example, 7 is −7, because 7 + (−7) = 0, and the _____ of −0.3 is 0.3, because −0.3 + 0.3 = 0.
a. Additive inverse0
b. Thing
c. Undefined
d. Undefined

26. In mathematics, the _____ (or modulus) of a real number is its numerical value without regard to its sign.
a. Absolute value0
b. Thing
c. Undefined
d. Undefined

27. A _____ is a negotiable instrument instructing a financial institution to pay a specific amount of a specific currency from a specific demand account held in the maker/depositor's name with that institution. Both the maker and payee may be natural persons or legal entities.
a. Check0
b. Thing
c. Undefined
d. Undefined

28. A frame of _____ is a particular perspective from which the universe is observed.
a. Thing
b. Reference0
c. Undefined
d. Undefined

29. The _____ of a function is an extension of the concept of a sum, and are identified or found through the use of integration.

Chapter 7. Another Look at Factoring Polynomials

a. Thing
c. Undefined
b. Integral0
d. Undefined

30. A _____ is a symbolic representation denoting a quantity or expression. It often represents an "unknown" quantity that has the potential to change.
    a. Thing
    b. Variable0
    c. Undefined
    d. Undefined

31. A _____ is a three-dimensional solid object bounded by six square faces, facets, or sides, with three meeting at each vertex.
    a. Thing
    b. Cube0
    c. Undefined
    d. Undefined

32. _____ are of a number n in its third power-the result of multiplying it by itself three times.
    a. Cubes0
    b. Thing
    c. Undefined
    d. Undefined

33. In plane geometry, a _____ is a polygon with four equal sides, four right angles, and parallel opposite sides. In algebra, the _____ of a number is that number multiplied by itself.
    a. Square0
    b. Thing
    c. Undefined
    d. Undefined

34. The term _____ can refer to an integer which is the square of some other integer, or an algebraic expression that can be factored as the square of some other expression.
    a. Perfect square0
    b. Thing
    c. Undefined
    d. Undefined

35. _____ was a French lawyer and a mathematician who is given credit for early developments that led to modern calculus. In particular, he is recognized for his discovery of an original method of finding the greatest and the smallest ordinates of curved lines, which is analogous to that of the then unknown differential calculus.
    a. Pierre de Fermat0
    b. Person
    c. Undefined
    d. Undefined

36. In mathematics, a _____ is a statement that can be proved on the basis of explicitly stated or previously agreed assumptions.
    a. Thing
    b. Theorem0
    c. Undefined
    d. Undefined

37. _____ is a relation in Euclidean geometry among the three sides of a right triangle.
    a. Pythagorean Theorem0
    b. Thing
    c. Undefined
    d. Undefined

38. In geographic information systems, a _____ comprises an entity with a geographic location, typically determined by points, arcs, or polygons. Carriageways and cadastres exemplify _____ data.

Chapter 7. Another Look at Factoring Polynomials

    a. Thing
    c. Undefined
    b. Feature0
    d. Undefined

39. Sir _____ is a British-American research mathematician at Princeton University, specializing in number theory.
    a. Andrew Wiles0
    b. Person
    c. Undefined
    d. Undefined

40. In mathematics the _____ refers to the identity: $a^2 - b^2 = (a+b)(a-b)$
    a. Difference of two squares0
    b. Thing
    c. Undefined
    d. Undefined

41. In mathematics, an inequality is a statement about the relative size or order of two objects. For example 14 > 10, or 14 is _____ 10.
    a. Greater than0
    b. Thing
    c. Undefined
    d. Undefined

42. In common philosophical language, a proposition or _____, is the content of an assertion, that is, it is true-or-false and defined by the meaning of a particular piece of language.
    a. Concept
    b. Statement0
    c. Undefined
    d. Undefined

43. In mathematics, there are several meanings of _____ depending on the subject.
    a. Degree0
    b. Thing
    c. Undefined
    d. Undefined

44. The mathematical concept of a _____ expresses the intuitive idea of deterministic dependence between two quantities, one of which is viewed as primary and the other as secondary. A _____ then is a way to associate a unique output for each input of a specified type, for example, a real number or an element of a given set.
    a. Function0
    b. Thing
    c. Undefined
    d. Undefined

45. A _____ of a number is a number a such that $a^3 = x$.
    a. Thing
    b. Cube root0
    c. Undefined
    d. Undefined

46. In mathematics, a _____ of a complex-valued function f is a member x of the domain of f such that f(x) vanishes at x, that is, x : f (x) = 0.
    a. Thing
    b. Root0
    c. Undefined
    d. Undefined

47. A _____ is a number which is the cube of an integer.
    a. Thing
    b. Perfect cube0
    c. Undefined
    d. Undefined

48. _____, either of the curved-bracket punctuation marks that together make a set of _____

Chapter 7. Another Look at Factoring Polynomials

a. Parentheses0
b. Thing
c. Undefined
d. Undefined

49. _____ the expected value of a random variable displays the average or central value of the variable. It is a summary value of the distribution of the variable.
   a. Determining0
   b. Thing
   c. Undefined
   d. Undefined

50. An _____ is a combination of numbers, operators, grouping symbols and/or free variables and bound variables arranged in a meaningful way which can be evaluated..
   a. Expression0
   b. Thing
   c. Undefined
   d. Undefined

51. In mathematics, a _____ can mean either an element of the set {1, 2, 3, ...} (i.e the positive integers or the counting numbers) or an element of the set {0, 1, 2, 3, ...} (i.e. the non-negative integers).
   a. Thing
   b. Natural number0
   c. Undefined
   d. Undefined

52. In mathematics, a _____ is a polynomial equation of the second degree. The general form is $ax^2 + bx + c = 0$.
   a. Thing
   b. Quadratic equation0
   c. Undefined
   d. Undefined

53. A _____ is a polynomial function of the form $f(x) = ax^2 + bx + c$, where a, b, c are real numbers and a , 0.
   a. Event
   b. Quadratic function0
   c. Undefined
   d. Undefined

54. In mathematics, an _____ is a statement about the relative size or order of two objects.
   a. Inequality0
   b. Thing
   c. Undefined
   d. Undefined

55. A quadratic equation with real solutions, called roots, which may be real or complex, is given by the _____: $x = \frac{-b \pm \sqrt{b^2 - 4ac}}{2a}$.
   a. Quadratic formula0
   b. Thing
   c. Undefined
   d. Undefined

56. A _____ is an equation in which each term is either a constant or the product of a constant times the first power of a variable.
   a. Thing
   b. Linear equation0
   c. Undefined
   d. Undefined

57. _____ is a notation for writing numbers that is often used by scientists and mathematicians to make it easier to write large and small numbers.
   a. Scientific notation0
   b. Thing
   c. Undefined
   d. Undefined

Chapter 7. Another Look at Factoring Polynomials

58. A _____ signifies a point or points of probability on a subject e.g., the _____ of creativity, which allows for the formation of rule or norm or law by interpretation of the phenomena events that can be created.
   a. Thing
   b. Principle0
   c. Undefined
   d. Undefined

59. Equivalence is the condition of being _____ or essentially equal.
   a. Thing
   b. Equivalent0
   c. Undefined
   d. Undefined

60. _____ is a branch of mathematics concerning the study of structure, relation and quantity.
   a. Concept
   b. Algebra0
   c. Undefined
   d. Undefined

61. In mathematics, the _____ is a conic section generated by the intersection of a right circular conical surface and a plane parallel to a generating straight line of that surface. It can also be defined as locus of points in a plane which are equidistant from a given point.
   a. Thing
   b. Parabola0
   c. Undefined
   d. Undefined

62. In geometry, a _____ is a special kind of point, usually a corner of a polygon, polyhedron, or higher dimensional polytope. In the geometry of curves a _____ is a point of where the first derivative of curvature is zero. In graph theory, a _____ is the fundamental unit out of which graphs are formed
   a. Vertex0
   b. Thing
   c. Undefined
   d. Undefined

63. In mathematics, an _____ number is a complex number whose square is a negative real number. They were defined in 1572 by Rafael Bombelli.
   a. Thing
   b. Imaginary0
   c. Undefined
   d. Undefined

64. In mathematics, an _____ number is any real number that is not a rational number- that is, it is a number which cannot be expressed as a fraction m/n, where m and n are integers.
   a. Irrational0
   b. Thing
   c. Undefined
   d. Undefined

65. In geometry, a _____ is defined as a quadrilateral where all four of its angles are right angles.
   a. Rectangle0
   b. Thing
   c. Undefined
   d. Undefined

66. The metre (or _____, see spelling differences) is a measure of length. It is the basic unit of length in the metric system and in the International System of Units (SI), used around the world for general and scientific purposes.
   a. Concept
   b. Meter0
   c. Undefined
   d. Undefined

Chapter 7. Another Look at Factoring Polynomials

67. _____ is the distance around a given two-dimensional object. As a general rule, the _____ of a polygon can always be calculated by adding all the length of the sides together. So, the formula for triangles is P = a + b + c, where a, b and c stand for each side of it. For quadrilaterals the equation is P = a + b + c + d. For equilateral polygons, P = na, where n is the number of sides and a is the side length.
    a. Thing
    b. Perimeter0
    c. Undefined
    d. Undefined

68. In mathematics, a _____ is a polynomial equation of the third degree.
    a. Thing
    b. Cubic equation0
    c. Undefined
    d. Undefined

Chapter 8. Radical Expressions, Complex Numbers, and Quadratic Equations

1. The _____ of a solid object is the three-dimensional concept of how much space it occupies, often quantified numerically.
   a. Thing
   b. Volume0
   c. Undefined
   d. Undefined

2. _____ is the design, analysis, and/or construction of works for practical purposes.
   a. Thing
   b. Engineering0
   c. Undefined
   d. Undefined

3. _____ is a mathematical operation, written a^n, involving two numbers, the base a and the exponent n.
   a. Thing
   b. Exponentiating0
   c. Undefined
   d. Undefined

4. _____ is a mathematical operation, written a^n, involving two numbers, the base a and the exponent n.
   a. Thing
   b. Exponentiation0
   c. Undefined
   d. Undefined

5. In Euclidean geometry, a uniform _____ is a linear transformation that enlargers or diminishes objects, and whose _____ factor is the same in all directions. This is also called homothethy.
   a. Thing
   b. Scale0
   c. Undefined
   d. Undefined

6. A _____ is a function that assigns a number to subsets of a given set.
   a. Thing
   b. Measure0
   c. Undefined
   d. Undefined

7. _____ is the symbol used to indicate the nth root of a number
   a. Thing
   b. Radical0
   c. Undefined
   d. Undefined

8. In mathematics, _____ are used to indicate the square root of a number.
   a. Radicals0
   b. Thing
   c. Undefined
   d. Undefined

9. In mathematics, a _____ number is a number which can be expressed as a ratio of two integers. Non-integer _____ numbers (commonly called fractions) are usually written as the vulgar fraction a / b, where b is not zero.
   a. Rational0
   b. Thing
   c. Undefined
   d. Undefined

10. In mathematics, a _____ is the result of multiplying, or an expression that identifies factors to be multiplied.
    a. Product0
    b. Thing
    c. Undefined
    d. Undefined

11. In plane geometry, a _____ is a polygon with four equal sides, four right angles, and parallel opposite sides. In algebra, the _____ of a number is that number multiplied by itself.

Chapter 8. Radical Expressions, Complex Numbers, and Quadratic Equations

    a. Thing
    c. Undefined
    b. Square0
    d. Undefined

12. In mathematics, a _____ of a number x is a number r such that r^2 = x, or in words, a number r whose square (the result of multiplying the number by itself) is x.
    a. Thing
    c. Undefined
    b. Square root0
    d. Undefined

13. In mathematics, a _____ of a complex-valued function f is a member x of the domain of f such that f(x) vanishes at x, that is, x : f (x) = 0.
    a. Root0
    c. Undefined
    b. Thing
    d. Undefined

14. _____ are the basic objects of study in graph theory. Informally speaking, a graph is a set of objects called points, nodes, or vertices connected by links called lines or edges.
    a. Graphs0
    c. Undefined
    b. Thing
    d. Undefined

15. The mathematical concept of a _____ expresses the intuitive idea of deterministic dependence between two quantities, one of which is viewed as primary and the other as secondary. A _____ then is a way to associate a unique output for each input of a specified type, for example, a real number or an element of a given set.
    a. Function0
    c. Undefined
    b. Thing
    d. Undefined

16. _____ has many meanings, most of which simply .
    a. Power0
    c. Undefined
    b. Thing
    d. Undefined

17. _____ is a method for differentiating expressions involving exponentiation the power operation.
    a. Thing
    c. Undefined
    b. Power rule0
    d. Undefined

18. An _____ of a number *a* is a number *b* such that b^n=a.
    a. Thing
    c. Undefined
    b. Nth root0
    d. Undefined

19. An _____ is a combination of numbers, operators, grouping symbols and/or free variables and bound variables arranged in a meaningful way which can be evaluated..
    a. Thing
    c. Undefined
    b. Expression0
    d. Undefined

20. Mathematical _____ is used to represent ideas.
    a. Notation0
    c. Undefined
    b. Thing
    d. Undefined

21. The _____ is the number or expression underneath the radical sign.

a. Radicand0 b. Thing
c. Undefined d. Undefined

22. The word _____ is used in a variety of ways in mathematics.
a. Thing b. Index0
c. Undefined d. Undefined

23. In mathematics, a _____ may be described informally as a number that can be given by an infinite decimal representation.
a. Thing b. Real number0
c. Undefined d. Undefined

24. In mathematics, a _____ is a number which can be expressed as a ratio of two integers. Non-integer rational numbers (commonly called fractions) are usually written as the vulgar fraction a / b, where b is not zero.
a. Rational Number0 b. Concept
c. Undefined d. Undefined

25. In mathematics, _____ growth occurs when the growth rate of a function is always proportional to the function's current size.
a. Exponential0 b. Thing
c. Undefined d. Undefined

26. _____ is a notation for writing numbers that is often used by scientists and mathematicians to make it easier to write large and small numbers.
a. Scientific notation0 b. Thing
c. Undefined d. Undefined

27. The _____, the average in everyday English, which is also called the arithmetic _____ (and is distinguished from the geometric _____ or harmonic _____). The average is also called the sample _____. The expected value of a random variable, which is also called the population _____.
a. Mean0 b. Thing
c. Undefined d. Undefined

28. _____, either of the curved-bracket punctuation marks that together make a set of _____
a. Parentheses0 b. Thing
c. Undefined d. Undefined

29. The _____ (symbol _____) and the millibar (symbol mbar, also mb) are units of pressure.
a. Bar0 b. Thing
c. Undefined d. Undefined

30. The _____ of a function is an extension of the concept of a sum, and are identified or found through the use of integration.
a. Thing b. Integral0
c. Undefined d. Undefined

Chapter 8. Radical Expressions, Complex Numbers, and Quadratic Equations

31. A _____ is a symbolic representation denoting a quantity or expression. It often represents an "unknown" quantity that has the potential to change.
   a. Variable0
   b. Thing
   c. Undefined
   d. Undefined

32. In mathematics, and in particular in abstract algebra, the _____ is a property of binary operations that generalises the distributive law from elementary algebra.
   a. Thing
   b. Distributive property0
   c. Undefined
   d. Undefined

33. In mathematics, factorization (British English: factorisation) or factoring is the decomposition of an object (for example, a number, a polynomial, or a matrix) into a product of other objects, or _____, which when multiplied together give the original.
   a. Factors0
   b. Thing
   c. Undefined
   d. Undefined

34. A _____ is the result of the addition of a set of numbers. The numbers may be natural numbers, complex numbers, matrices, or still more complicated objects. An infinite _____ is a subtle procedure known as a series.
   a. Thing
   b. Sum0
   c. Undefined
   d. Undefined

35. A _____ is a three-dimensional solid object bounded by six square faces, facets, or sides, with three meeting at each vertex.
   a. Cube0
   b. Thing
   c. Undefined
   d. Undefined

36. _____ are of a number n in its third power-the result of multiplying it by itself three times.
   a. Cubes0
   b. Thing
   c. Undefined
   d. Undefined

37. A _____ is a number that is less than zero.
   a. Thing
   b. Negative number0
   c. Undefined
   d. Undefined

38. In mathematics, a _____ is any one of several different types of functions, mappings, operations, or transformations.
   a. Projection0
   b. Thing
   c. Undefined
   d. Undefined

39. In mathematics, a _____ of a k-place relation $L \subseteq X_1 \times \ldots \times X_k$ is one of the sets X_j, $1 \leq j \leq k$. In the special case where k = 2 and $L \subseteq X_1 \times X_2$ is a function $L : X_1 \to X_2$, it is conventional to refer to X_1 as the _____ of the function and to refer to X_2 as the codomain of the function.
   a. Thing
   b. Domain0
   c. Undefined
   d. Undefined

Chapter 8. Radical Expressions, Complex Numbers, and Quadratic Equations

40. In mathematics, a _____ can mean either an element of the set {1, 2, 3, ...} (i.e the positive integers or the counting numbers) or an element of the set {0, 1, 2, 3, ...} (i.e. the non-negative integers).
   a. Natural number0
   b. Thing
   c. Undefined
   d. Undefined

41. In mathematics, _____ is an elementary arithmetic operation. When one of the numbers is a whole number, _____ is the repeated sum of the other number.
   a. Multiplication0
   b. Thing
   c. Undefined
   d. Undefined

42. In mathematics, defined and _____ are used to explain whether or not expressions have meaningful, sensible, and unambiguous values.
   a. Thing
   b. Undefined0
   c. Undefined
   d. Undefined

43. In mathematics, a _____ is an expression that is constructed from one or more variables and constants, using only the operations of addition, subtraction, multiplication, and constant positive whole number exponents. is a _____. Note in particular that division by an expression containing a variable is not in general allowed in polynomials. [1]
   a. Polynomial0
   b. Thing
   c. Undefined
   d. Undefined

44. In mathematics, a _____ is a constant multiplicative factor of a certain object. The object can be such things as a variable, a vector, a function, etc. For example, the _____ of $9x^2$ is 9.
   a. Thing
   b. Coefficient0
   c. Undefined
   d. Undefined

45. A _____ of a number is a number a such that $a^3 = x$.
   a. Cube root0
   b. Thing
   c. Undefined
   d. Undefined

46. In mathematics, a _____ is the end result of a division problem. It can also be expressed as the number of times the divisor divides into the dividend.
   a. Quotient0
   b. Thing
   c. Undefined
   d. Undefined

47. In mathematics, _____ expressions is used to reduce the expression into the lowest possible term.
   a. Thing
   b. Simplifying0
   c. Undefined
   d. Undefined

48. A _____ is a number which is the cube of an integer.
   a. Perfect cube0
   b. Thing
   c. Undefined
   d. Undefined

49. The term _____ can refer to an integer which is the square of some other integer, or an algebraic expression that can be factored as the square of some other expression.

Chapter 8. Radical Expressions, Complex Numbers, and Quadratic Equations 99

    a. Perfect square0
    c. Undefined
    b. Thing
    d. Undefined

50. A _____ is the part of a fraction that tells how many equal parts make up a whole, and which is used in the name of the fraction: "halves", "thirds", "fourths" or "quarters", "fifths" and so on.
    a. Denominator0
    c. Undefined
    b. Concept
    d. Undefined

51. A _____ is a numeral used to indicate a count. The most common use of the word today is to name the part of a fraction that tells the number or count of equal parts.
    a. Numerator0
    c. Undefined
    b. Thing
    d. Undefined

52. A _____ is a negotiable instrument instructing a financial institution to pay a specific amount of a specific currency from a specific demand account held in the maker/depositor's name with that institution. Both the maker and payee may be natural persons or legal entities.
    a. Thing
    c. Undefined
    b. Check0
    d. Undefined

53. In mathematics, an _____ number is any real number that is not a rational number- that is, it is a number which cannot be expressed as a fraction m/n, where m and n are integers.
    a. Irrational0
    c. Undefined
    b. Thing
    d. Undefined

54. In mathematics, an _____ is any real number that is not a rational number ¡ª that is, it is a number which cannot be expressed as m/n, where m and n are integers.
    a. Thing
    c. Undefined
    b. Irrational number0
    d. Undefined

55. In mathematics, _____ are any real number that is not a rational number ¡ª that is, it is a number which cannot be expressed as m/n, where m and n are integers.
    a. Irrational numbers0
    c. Undefined
    b. Thing
    d. Undefined

56. In mathematics, the _____ (or modulus) of a real number is its numerical value without regard to its sign.
    a. Absolute value0
    c. Undefined
    b. Thing
    d. Undefined

57. The act of _____ is the calculated approximation of a result which is usable even if input data may be incomplete, uncertain, or noisy.
    a. Estimating0
    c. Undefined
    b. Thing
    d. Undefined

58. In common philosophical language, a proposition or _____, is the content of an assertion, that is, it is true-or-false and defined by the meaning of a particular piece of language.

Chapter 8. Radical Expressions, Complex Numbers, and Quadratic Equations

    a. Statement0
    b. Concept
    c. Undefined
    d. Undefined

59. A _____ is one of the basic shapes of geometry: a polygon with three vertices and three sides which are straight line segments.
    a. Triangle0
    b. Thing
    c. Undefined
    d. Undefined

60. The _____ of a right triangle is the triangle's longest side; the side opposite the right angle.
    a. Hypotenuse0
    b. Thing
    c. Undefined
    d. Undefined

61. _____ has one 90° internal angle a right angle.
    a. Thing
    b. Right triangle0
    c. Undefined
    d. Undefined

62. A _____ can refer to a line joining two nonadjacent vertices of a polygon or polyhedron, or in some contexts any upward or downward sloping line. .
    a. Diagonal0
    b. Thing
    c. Undefined
    d. Undefined

63. In algebra, a _____ is a binomial formed by taking the opposite of the second term of a binomial.
    a. Thing
    b. Conjugate0
    c. Undefined
    d. Undefined

64. _____, or Rationalisation in mathematics is the process of removing a square root or imaginary number from the denominator of a fraction.
    a. Thing
    b. Rationalizing0
    c. Undefined
    d. Undefined

65. In mathematics, the _____ inverse of a number x, denoted $1/x$ or x^{-1}, is the number which, when multiplied by x, yields 1. The _____ inverse of x is also called the reciprocal of x.
    a. Multiplicative0
    b. Thing
    c. Undefined
    d. Undefined

66. An _____ is an equality that remains true regardless of the values of any variables that appear within it, to distinguish it from an equality which is true under more particular conditions.
    a. Identity0
    b. Thing
    c. Undefined
    d. Undefined

67. In mathematics, a _____ is a polynomial equation of the second degree. The general form is $ax^2 + bx + c = 0$.
    a. Thing
    b. Quadratic equation0
    c. Undefined
    d. Undefined

68. The _____ integers are all the integers from zero on upwards.

Chapter 8. Radical Expressions, Complex Numbers, and Quadratic Equations

a. Thing
c. Undefined
b. Nonnegative0
d. Undefined

69. In Euclidean geometry, a _____ is the set of all points in a plane at a fixed distance, called the radius, from a given point, the center.
    a. Thing
    c. Undefined
    b. Circle0
    d. Undefined

70. A _____ is a quantity that denotes the proportional amount or magnitude of one quantity relative to another.
    a. Thing
    c. Undefined
    b. Ratio0
    d. Undefined

71. _____ is the distance around a given two-dimensional object. As a general rule, the _____ of a polygon can always be calculated by adding all the length of the sides together. So, the formula for triangles is P = a + b + c, where a, b and c stand for each side of it. For quadrilaterals the equation is P = a + b + c + d. For equilateral polygons, P = na, where n is the number of sides and a is the side length.
    a. Perimeter0
    c. Undefined
    b. Thing
    d. Undefined

72. In mathematics, a _____ is a number in the form of a + bi where a and b are real numbers, and i is the imaginary unit, with the property i 2 = −1. The real number a is called the real part of the _____, and the real number b is the imaginary part.
    a. Complex number0
    c. Undefined
    b. Thing
    d. Undefined

73. In mathematics, an _____ number is a complex number whose square is a negative real number. They were defined in 1572 by Rafael Bombelli.
    a. Imaginary0
    c. Undefined
    b. Thing
    d. Undefined

74. In mathematics, the _____ i (or sometimes the Latin j or the Greek iota, see below) allows the real number system R to be extended to the complex number system C. Its precise definition is dependent upon the particular method of extension.
    a. Imaginary unit0
    c. Undefined
    b. Thing
    d. Undefined

75. An _____ or member of a set is an object that when collected together make up the set.
    a. Element0
    c. Undefined
    b. Thing
    d. Undefined

76. In mathematics, the _____ , or members of a set or more generally a class are all those objects which when collected together make up the set or class.
    a. Thing
    c. Undefined
    b. Elements0
    d. Undefined

77. A _____ is a set whose members are members of another set or a set contained within another set.

Chapter 8. Radical Expressions, Complex Numbers, and Quadratic Equations

a. Thing
b. Subset0
c. Undefined
d. Undefined

78. _____ are groups whose members are members of another set or a set contained within another set.
a. Thing
b. Subsets0
c. Undefined
d. Undefined

79. In statistics, _____ means the most frequent value assumed by a random variable, or occurring in a sampling of a random variable.
a. Mode0
b. Concept
c. Undefined
d. Undefined

80. Two mathematical objects are equal if and only if they are precisely the same in every way. This defines a binary relation, _____, denoted by the sign of _____ "=" in such a way that the statement "x = y" means that x and y are equal.
a. Equality0
b. Thing
c. Undefined
d. Undefined

81. _____ or arithmetics is the oldest and most elementary branch of mathematics, used by almost everyone, for tasks ranging from simple daily counting to advanced science and business calculations.
a. Thing
b. Arithmetic0
c. Undefined
d. Undefined

82. In elementary algebra, a _____ is a polynomial with two terms: the sum of two monomials. It is the simplest kind of polynomial except for a monomial.
a. Binomial0
b. Thing
c. Undefined
d. Undefined

83. A _____ of a number is the product of that number with any integer.
a. Thing
b. Multiple0
c. Undefined
d. Undefined

84. In mathematics the _____ refers to the identity: $a^2 - b^2 = (a+b)(a-b)$
a. Difference of two squares0
b. Thing
c. Undefined
d. Undefined

85. Leonhard _____ was a pioneering Swiss mathematician and physicist, who spent most of his life in Russia and Germany.
a. Euler0
b. Person
c. Undefined
d. Undefined

86. In geographic information systems, a _____ comprises an entity with a geographic location, typically determined by points, arcs, or polygons. Carriageways and cadastres exemplify _____ data.
a. Thing
b. Feature0
c. Undefined
d. Undefined

Chapter 8. Radical Expressions, Complex Numbers, and Quadratic Equations

87. In mathematics, the _____ of a complex number z, is the first element of the ordered pair of real numbers representing z, i.e. if z = (x,y), or equivalently, z = x + iy, then the _____ of z is x. It is denoted by Re{z} . The complex function which maps z to the _____ of z is not holomorphic.
   a. Thing
   b. Real part0
   c. Undefined
   d. Undefined

88. A quadratic equation with real solutions, called roots, which may be real or complex, is given by the _____: $x = \frac{-b \pm \sqrt{b^2 - 4ac}}{2a}$.
   a. Quadratic formula0
   b. Thing
   c. Undefined
   d. Undefined

89. In mathematics, an _____ is a statement about the relative size or order of two objects.
   a. Inequality0
   b. Thing
   c. Undefined
   d. Undefined

90. _____ of a polynomial with real or complex coefficients is a certain expression in the coefficients of the polynomial which is equal to zero if and only if the polynomial has a multiple root i.e. a root with multiplicity greater than one in the complex numbers.
   a. Thing
   b. Discriminant0
   c. Undefined
   d. Undefined

91. In mathematics, _____ is the decomposition of an object into a product of other objects, or factors, which when multiplied together give the original.
   a. Factoring0
   b. Thing
   c. Undefined
   d. Undefined

92. The plus and _____ signs are mathematical symbols used to represent the notions of positive and negative as well as the operations of addition and subtraction.
   a. Thing
   b. Minus0
   c. Undefined
   d. Undefined

93. The _____ are the only integral domain whose positive elements are well-ordered, and in which order is preserved by addition. Like the natural numbers, the _____ form a countably infinite set. The set of all _____ is usually denoted in mathematics by a boldface Z .
   a. ThIng
   b. Integers0
   c. Undefined
   d. Undefined

94. A _____ is a polynomial function of the form $f(x) = ax^2 + bx + c$, where a, b, c are real numbers and a , 0.
   a. Event
   b. Quadratic function0
   c. Undefined
   d. Undefined

95. Equivalence is the condition of being _____ or essentially equal.
   a. Thing
   b. Equivalent0
   c. Undefined
   d. Undefined

Chapter 8. Radical Expressions, Complex Numbers, and Quadratic Equations

96. In mathematics, the _____ is a conic section generated by the intersection of a right circular conical surface and a plane parallel to a generating straight line of that surface. It can also be defined as locus of points in a plane which are equidistant from a given point.
   a. Parabola0
   b. Thing
   c. Undefined
   d. Undefined

97. _____ is a technique used in algebra to solve quadratic equations, in analytic geometry for determining the shapes of graphs, and in calculus for computing integrals, including, but hardly limited to, the integrals that define Laplace transforms. The essential objective is to reduce a quadratic polynomial in a variable in an equation or expression to a squared polynomial of linear order. This can reduce an equation or integral to one that is more easily solved or evaluated.
   a. Thing
   b. Completing the square0
   c. Undefined
   d. Undefined

98. Mathematical _____ really refers to two distinct areas of research: the first is the application of the techniques of formal _____ to mathematics and mathematical reasoning, and the second, in the other direction, the application of mathematical techniques to the representation and analysis of formal _____.
   a. Thing
   b. Logic0
   c. Undefined
   d. Undefined

99. In mathematics, a _____ is a countable collection of open covers of a topological space that satisfies certain separation axioms.
   a. Thing
   b. Development0
   c. Undefined
   d. Undefined

100. In mathematics and the mathematical sciences, a _____ is a fixed, but possibly unspecified, value. This is in contrast to a variable, which is not fixed.
   a. Constant0
   b. Thing
   c. Undefined
   d. Undefined

101. The word _____ comes from the Latin word linearis, which means created by lines.
   a. Linear0
   b. Thing
   c. Undefined
   d. Undefined

102. A _____ is an equation in which each term is either a constant or the product of a constant times the first power of a variable.
   a. Linear equation0
   b. Thing
   c. Undefined
   d. Undefined

103. A _____ is a set of numbers that designate location in a given reference system, such as x,y in a planar _____ system or an x,y,z in a three-dimensional _____ system.
   a. Coordinate0
   b. Thing
   c. Undefined
   d. Undefined

104. In mathematics, a _____ is a two-dimensional manifold or surface that is perfectly flat.

Chapter 8. Radical Expressions, Complex Numbers, and Quadratic Equations

a. Plane0
b. Thing
c. Undefined
d. Undefined

105. _____ was an English mathematician.
a. Thing
b. James Joseph Sylvester0
c. Undefined
d. Undefined

106. In geometry, a _____ is a special kind of point, usually a corner of a polygon, polyhedron, or higher dimensional polytope. In the geometry of curves a _____ is a point of where the first derivative of curvature is zero. In graph theory, a _____ is the fundamental unit out of which graphs are formed
a. Vertex0
b. Thing
c. Undefined
d. Undefined

107. In mathematics, the _____ of a complex number z, is the second element of the ordered pair of real numbers representing z, i.e. if z = (x,y), or equivalently, z = x + iy, then the _____ of z is y.
a. Thing
b. Imaginary part0
c. Undefined
d. Undefined

108. In mathematics, an inequality is a statement about the relative size or order of two objects. For example 14 > 10, or 14 is _____ 10.
a. Thing
b. Greater than0
c. Undefined
d. Undefined

109. A _____ is a polynomial consisting of three terms; in other words, it is the sum of three monomials.
a. Thing
b. Trinomial0
c. Undefined
d. Undefined

110. In geometry, a _____ is defined as a quadrilateral where all four of its angles are right angles.
a. Rectangle0
b. Thing
c. Undefined
d. Undefined

111. In mathematics, a _____ is a demonstration that, assuming certain axioms, some statement is necessarily true.
a. Thing
b. Proof0
c. Undefined
d. Undefined

112. _____ variables are variables other than the independent variable that may bear any effect on the behavior of the subject being studied.
a. Extraneous0
b. Thing
c. Undefined
d. Undefined

113. In mathematics, the _____ of two sets A and B is the set that contains all elements of A that also belong to B (or equivalently, all elements of B that also belong to A), but no other elements.
a. Thing
b. Intersection0
c. Undefined
d. Undefined

Chapter 8. Radical Expressions, Complex Numbers, and Quadratic Equations

114. _____ is a relation in Euclidean geometry among the three sides of a right triangle.
   a. Thing
   b. Pythagorean Theorem0
   c. Undefined
   d. Undefined

115. In mathematics, a _____ is a statement that can be proved on the basis of explicitly stated or previously agreed assumptions.
   a. Theorem0
   b. Thing
   c. Undefined
   d. Undefined

116. In geometry, two lines or planes if one falls on the other in such a way as to create congruent adjacent angles. The term may be used as a noun or adjective. Thus, referring to Figure 1, the line AB is the _____ to CD through the point B.
   a. Perpendicular0
   b. Thing
   c. Undefined
   d. Undefined

117. In a right triangle, the _____ of the triangle are the two sides that are perpendicular to each other, as opposed to the hypotenuse.
   a. Thing
   b. Legs0
   c. Undefined
   d. Undefined

118. _____ is the branch of pure mathematics concerned with the properties of numbers in general, and integers in particular, as well as the wider classes of problems that arise from their study.
   a. Number theory0
   b. Thing
   c. Undefined
   d. Undefined

119. In _____ algebra, a *-ring is an associative ring with an antilinear, antiautomorphism * : A ¨ A which is an involution.
   a. Star0
   b. Thing
   c. Undefined
   d. Undefined

120. In geometry, a _____ is any five-sided polygon.
   a. Pentagon0
   b. Thing
   c. Undefined
   d. Undefined

121. _____ Logic is a concept in traditional logic referring to a "type of immediate inference in which from a given proposition another proposition is inferred which has as its subject the predicate of the original proposition and as its predicate the subject of the original proposition (the quality of the proposition being retained)."
   a. Concept
   b. Converse0
   c. Undefined
   d. Undefined

122. _____ is electromagnetic radiation with a wavelength that is visible to the eye (visible _____) or, in a technical or scientific context, electromagnetic radiation of any wavelength.
   a. Thing
   b. Light0
   c. Undefined
   d. Undefined

123. In mathematics, the _____ of a function is the set of all "output" values produced by that function. Given a function $f : A \to B$, the _____ of f, is defined to be the set $\{x \in B : x = f(a) \text{ for some } a \in A\}$.

Chapter 8. Radical Expressions, Complex Numbers, and Quadratic Equations

a. Range0
b. Thing
c. Undefined
d. Undefined

124. In astronomy, geography, geometry and related sciences and contexts, a plane is said to be _____ at a given point if it is locally perpendicular to the gradient of the gravity field, i.e., with the direction of the gravitational force at that point.
a. Thing
b. Horizontal0
c. Undefined
d. Undefined

125. _____ is the art and science of designing buildings and structures.
a. Thing
b. Architecture0
c. Undefined
d. Undefined

126. Compass and straightedge or ruler-and-compass _____ is the _____ of lengths or angles using only an idealized ruler and compass.
a. Thing
b. Construction0
c. Undefined
d. Undefined

127. The _____ of measurement are a globally standardized and modernized form of the metric system.
a. Thing
b. Units0
c. Undefined
d. Undefined

128. A frame of _____ is a particular perspective from which the universe is observed.
a. Reference0
b. Thing
c. Undefined
d. Undefined

129. The metre (or _____, see spelling differences) is a measure of length. It is the basic unit of length in the metric system and in the International System of Units (SI), used around the world for general and scientific purposes.
a. Concept
b. Meter0
c. Undefined
d. Undefined

130. In geometry, the _____ of an object is a point in some sense in the middle of the object.
a. Thing
b. Center0
c. Undefined
d. Undefined

131. In business, _____, _____ cost or _____ expense refers to an ongoing expense of operating a business.
a. Overhead0
b. Thing
c. Undefined
d. Undefined

132. Sir Isaac _____, was an English physicist, mathematician, astronomer, natural philosopher, and alchemist, regarded by many as the greatest figure in the history of science
a. Person
b. Newton0
c. Undefined
d. Undefined

133. _____ is a branch of mathematics concerning the study of structure, relation and quantity.

Chapter 8. Radical Expressions, Complex Numbers, and Quadratic Equations

a. Concept
c. Undefined
b. Algebra0
d. Undefined

134. _____ means in succession or back-to-back
 a. Thing
 c. Undefined
 b. Consecutive0
 d. Undefined

135. In mathematics, the conjugate _____ or adjoint matrix of an m-by-n matrix A with complex entries is the n-by-m matrix A* obtained from A by taking the transpose and then taking the complex conjugate of each entry.
 a. Thing
 c. Undefined
 b. Pairs0
 d. Undefined

136. _____ over a given field is a polynomial with coefficients in that field.
 a. Thing
 c. Undefined
 b. Algebraic equation0
 d. Undefined

137. A _____ is a vehicle, missile or aircraft which obtains thrust by the reaction to the ejection of fast moving fluid from within a _____ engine.
 a. Rocket0
 c. Undefined
 b. Thing
 d. Undefined

138. _____ is the fee paid on borrowed money.
 a. Thing
 c. Undefined
 b. Interest0
 d. Undefined

139. _____ interest refers to the fact that whenever interest is calculated, it is based not only on the original principal, but also on any unpaid interest that has been added to the principal.
 a. Compound0
 c. Undefined
 b. Thing
 d. Undefined

140. _____ refers to the fact that whenever interest is calculated, it is based not only on the original principal, but also on any unpaid interest that has been added to the principal. The more frequently interest is compounded, the faster the balance grows.
 a. Concept
 c. Undefined
 b. Compound interest0
 d. Undefined

141. A _____ is a special kind of ratio, indicating a relationship between two measurements with different units, such as miles to gallons or cents to pounds.
 a. Thing
 c. Undefined
 b. Rate0
 d. Undefined

142. _____ is a kind of property which exists as magnitude or multitude. It is among the basic classes of things along with quality, substance, change, and relation.
 a. Amount0
 c. Undefined
 b. Thing
 d. Undefined

Chapter 8. Radical Expressions, Complex Numbers, and Quadratic Equations

143. An _____ is the fee paid on borrow money.
   a. Concept
   c. Undefined
   b. Interest rate0
   d. Undefined

144. _____ or investing is a term with several closely-related meanings in business management, finance and economics, related to saving or deferring consumption.
   a. Investment0
   c. Undefined
   b. Thing
   d. Undefined

145. In elementary algebra, an _____ is a set that contains every real number between two indicated numbers and may contain the two numbers themselves.
   a. Thing
   c. Undefined
   b. Interval0
   d. Undefined

146. _____, from Latin meaning "to make progress", is defined in two different ways. Pure economic _____ is the increase in wealth that an investor has from making an investment, taking into consideration all costs associated with that investment including the opportunity cost of capital.
   a. Thing
   c. Undefined
   b. Profit0
   d. Undefined

147. _____ are external two-dimensional outlines, with the appearance or configuration of some thing - in contrast to the matter or content or substance of which it is composed.
   a. Shapes0
   c. Undefined
   b. Thing
   d. Undefined

148. In mathematics, in the field of group theory, a _____ of a group is a quasisimple subnormal subgroup.
   a. Concept
   c. Undefined
   b. Component0
   d. Undefined

149. _____ the expected value of a random variable displays the average or central value of the variable. It is a summary value of the distribution of the variable.
   a. Determining0
   c. Undefined
   b. Thing
   d. Undefined

150. A _____ is a unit of length, usually used to measure distance, in a number of different systems, including Imperial units, United States customary units and Norwegian/Swedish mil. Its size can vary from system to system, but in each is between 1 and 10 kilometers. In contemporary English contexts _____ refers to either:
   a. Mile0
   c. Undefined
   b. Thing
   d. Undefined

151. _____ is a unit of speed, expressing the number of international miles covered per hour.
   a. Miles per hour0
   c. Undefined
   b. Thing
   d. Undefined

152. _____ is the transport of people on a trip/journey or the process or time involved in a person or object moving from one location to another.

Chapter 8. Radical Expressions, Complex Numbers, and Quadratic Equations

a. Travel0
b. Thing
c. Undefined
d. Undefined

153. In mathematics, _____ are two-dimensional manifolds or surfaces that are perfectly flat.
a. Thing
b. Planes0
c. Undefined
d. Undefined

154. _____ is a synonym for information.
a. Data0
b. Thing
c. Undefined
d. Undefined

155. In mathematics, an _____, mean, or central tendency of a data set refers to a measure of the "middle" or "expected" value of the data set.
a. Average0
b. Concept
c. Undefined
d. Undefined

156. In classical geometry, a _____ of a circle or sphere is any line segment from its center to its boundary. By extension, the _____ of a circle or sphere is the length of any such segment. The _____ is half the diameter. In science and engineering the term _____ of curvature is commonly used as a synonym for _____.
a. Radius0
b. Thing
c. Undefined
d. Undefined

157. In mathematics, suppose C is a collection of mathematical objects. Then we say that C is _____ if every $c \in C$ is uniquely determined by less information about c than one would expect.
a. Rigid0
b. Thing
c. Undefined
d. Undefined

158. _____ is a physical property of a system that underlies the common notions of hot and cold; something that is hotter has the greater _____.
a. Temperature0
b. Thing
c. Undefined
d. Undefined

159. In the mathematical field of numerical analysis, the _____ in some data is the discrepancy between an exact value and some approximation to it.
a. Thing
b. Approximation Error0
c. Undefined
d. Undefined

160. In geometry, a _____ (Greek words diairo = divide and metro = measure) of a circle is any straight line segment that passes through the centre and whose endpoints are on the circular boundary, or, in more modern usage, the length of such a line segment. When using the word in the more modern sense, one speaks of the _____ rather than a _____, because all diameters of a circle have the same length. This length is twice the radius. The _____ of a circle is also the longest chord that the circle has.
a. Thing
b. Diameter0
c. Undefined
d. Undefined

Chapter 8. Radical Expressions, Complex Numbers, and Quadratic Equations

161. In geometry, an _____ of a triangle is a straight line through a vertex and perpendicular to (i.e. forming a right angle with) the opposite side or an extension of the opposite side.
 a. Concept
 b. Altitude0
 c. Undefined
 d. Undefined

162. A _____ is a polygon with four sides and four vertices.
 a. Quadrilateral0
 b. Thing
 c. Undefined
 d. Undefined

163. _____ are procedures that allow people to exchange information by one of several methods.
 a. Thing
 b. Communications0
 c. Undefined
 d. Undefined

164. In geometry a _____ is a plane figure that is bounded by a closed path or circuit, composed of a finite number of sequential line segments.
 a. Polygon0
 b. Thing
 c. Undefined
 d. Undefined

165. In topology and related areas of mathematics a _____ or Moore-Smith sequence is a generalization of a sequence, intended to unify the various notions of limit and generalize them to arbitrary topological spaces.
 a. Thing
 b. Net0
 c. Undefined
 d. Undefined

166. A _____ is an instrument used in geometry technical drawing and engineering/building to measure distances and/or to rule straight lines.
 a. Thing
 b. Ruler0
 c. Undefined
 d. Undefined

167. In mathematics a _____ is a function which defines a distance between elements of a set.
 a. Metric0
 b. Thing
 c. Undefined
 d. Undefined

168. A _____ is an object that is attached to a pivot point so that it can swing freely.
 a. Pendulum0
 b. Thing
 c. Undefined
 d. Undefined

169. In business, particularly accounting, a _____ is the time intervals that the accounts, statement, payments, or other calculations cover.
 a. Period0
 b. Thing
 c. Undefined
 d. Undefined

170. Regrouping is the act of putting ones into groups of 10. For example, the 1 on the far right of 131 would be denoted _____ if the digit of the number being subtracted is larger than 1, such as 131-99.
 a. By 100
 b. Thing
 c. Undefined
 d. Undefined

171. In the scientific method, an _____ (Latin: ex-+-periri, "of (or from) trying"), is a set of actions and observations, performed in the context of solving a particular problem or question, in order to support or falsify a hypothesis or research concerning phenomena.
   a. Thing
   b. Experiment0
   c. Undefined
   d. Undefined

172. In mathematics, the concept of a _____ tries to capture the intuitive idea of a geometrical one-dimensional and continuous object. A simple example is the circle.
   a. Thing
   b. Curve0
   c. Undefined
   d. Undefined

Chapter 9. Rational Expressions

1. A _____ is a symbolic representation denoting a quantity or expression. It often represents an "unknown" quantity that has the potential to change.
   - a. Thing
   - b. Variable0
   - c. Undefined
   - d. Undefined

2. A _____ is the part of a fraction that tells how many equal parts make up a whole, and which is used in the name of the fraction: "halves", "thirds", "fourths" or "quarters", "fifths" and so on.
   - a. Denominator0
   - b. Concept
   - c. Undefined
   - d. Undefined

3. A _____ is a quantity that denotes the proportional amount or magnitude of one quantity relative to another.
   - a. Ratio0
   - b. Thing
   - c. Undefined
   - d. Undefined

4. In mathematics, a _____ number is a number which can be expressed as a ratio of two integers. Non-integer _____ numbers (commonly called fractions) are usually written as the vulgar fraction a / b, where b is not zero.
   - a. Rational0
   - b. Thing
   - c. Undefined
   - d. Undefined

5. An _____ is a combination of numbers, operators, grouping symbols and/or free variables and bound variables arranged in a meaningful way which can be evaluated..
   - a. Expression0
   - b. Thing
   - c. Undefined
   - d. Undefined

6. In mathematics, a _____ is an expression that is constructed from one or more variables and constants, using only the operations of addition, subtraction, multiplication, and constant positive whole number exponents. is a _____. Note in particular that division by an expression containing a variable is not in general allowed in polynomials. [1]
   - a. Thing
   - b. Polynomial0
   - c. Undefined
   - d. Undefined

7. In mathematics, a _____ is any function which can be written as the ratio of two polynomial functions.
   - a. Rational function0
   - b. Thing
   - c. Undefined
   - d. Undefined

8. The mathematical concept of a _____ expresses the intuitive idea of deterministic dependence between two quantities, one of which is viewed as primary and the other as secondary. A _____ then is a way to associate a unique output for each input of a specified type, for example, a real number or an element of a given set.
   - a. Function0
   - b. Thing
   - c. Undefined
   - d. Undefined

9. In mathematics, a _____ of a k-place relation $L \subseteq X_1 \times ... \times X_k$ is one of the sets X_j, $1 \leq j \leq k$. In the special case where k = 2 and $L \subseteq X_1 \times X_2$ is a function $L : X_1 \to X_2$, it is conventional to refer to X_1 as the _____ of the function and to refer to X_2 as the codomain of the function.
   - a. Thing
   - b. Domain0
   - c. Undefined
   - d. Undefined

10. In mathematics, a _____ is a particular kind of polynomial, having just one term.

Chapter 9. Rational Expressions

a. Monomial0
c. Undefined
b. Thing
d. Undefined

11. _____ is a mathematical operation, written a^n, involving two numbers, the base a and the exponent n.
   a. Thing
   b. Exponentiating0
   c. Undefined
   d. Undefined

12. _____ is a mathematical operation, written a^n, involving two numbers, the base a and the exponent n.
   a. Exponentiation0
   b. Thing
   c. Undefined
   d. Undefined

13. The _____ are the only integral domain whose positive elements are well-ordered, and in which order is preserved by addition. Like the natural numbers, the _____ form a countably infinite set. The set of all _____ is usually denoted in mathematics by a boldface Z .
   a. Integers0
   b. Thing
   c. Undefined
   d. Undefined

14. In mathematics, a _____ is the result of multiplying, or an expression that identifies factors to be multiplied.
   a. Product0
   b. Thing
   c. Undefined
   d. Undefined

15. In mathematics, a _____ may be described informally as a number that can be given by an infinite decimal representation.
   a. Thing
   b. Real number0
   c. Undefined
   d. Undefined

16. A _____ is the result of the addition of a set of numbers. The numbers may be natural numbers, complex numbers, matrices, or still more complicated objects. An infinite _____ is a subtle procedure known as a series.
   a. Thing
   b. Sum0
   c. Undefined
   d. Undefined

17. A _____ of a number is the product of that number with any integer.
   a. Thing
   b. Multiple0
   c. Undefined
   d. Undefined

18. _____ the expected value of a random variable displays the average or central value of the variable. It is a summary value of the distribution of the variable.
   a. Thing
   b. Determining0
   c. Undefined
   d. Undefined

19. In mathematics, defined and _____ are used to explain whether or not expressions have meaningful, sensible, and unambiguous values.
   a. Undefined0
   b. Thing
   c. Undefined
   d. Undefined

Chapter 9. Rational Expressions

20. A _____ is a negotiable instrument instructing a financial institution to pay a specific amount of a specific currency from a specific demand account held in the maker/depositor's name with that institution. Both the maker and payee may be natural persons or legal entities.
- a. Thing
- b. Check0
- c. Undefined
- d. Undefined

21. In mathematics, an _____ number is a complex number whose square is a negative real number. They were defined in 1572 by Rafael Bombelli.
- a. Thing
- b. Imaginary0
- c. Undefined
- d. Undefined

22. In mathematics, a _____ is any one of several different types of functions, mappings, operations, or transformations.
- a. Thing
- b. Projection0
- c. Undefined
- d. Undefined

23. An _____ is a straight line around which a geometric figure can be rotated.
- a. Thing
- b. Axis0
- c. Undefined
- d. Undefined

24. In mathematics, the _____ inverse of a number x, denoted 1/x or x^{-1}, is the number which, when multiplied by x, yields 1. The _____ inverse of x is also called the reciprocal of x.
- a. Multiplicative0
- b. Thing
- c. Undefined
- d. Undefined

25. A _____ signifies a point or points of probability on a subject e.g., the _____ of creativity, which allows for the formation of rule or norm or law by interpretation of the phenomena events that can be created.
- a. Thing
- b. Principle0
- c. Undefined
- d. Undefined

26. A _____ is a numeral used to indicate a count. The most common use of the word today is to name the part of a fraction that tells the number or count of equal parts.
- a. Thing
- b. Numerator0
- c. Undefined
- d. Undefined

27. _____ is the largest positive integer that divides both numbers without remainder.
- a. Thing
- b. Common Factor0
- c. Undefined
- d. Undefined

28. An _____ is an equality that remains true regardless of the values of any variables that appear within it, to distinguish it from an equality which is true under more particular conditions.
- a. Identity0
- b. Thing
- c. Undefined
- d. Undefined

29. In mathematics, factorization (British English: factorisation) or factoring is the decomposition of an object (for example, a number, a polynomial, or a matrix) into a product of other objects, or _____, which when multiplied together give the original.
a. Thing
b. Factors0
c. Undefined
d. Undefined

30. Two mathematical objects are equal if and only if they are precisely the same in every way. This defines a binary relation, _____, denoted by the sign of _____ "=" in such a way that the statement "x = y" means that x and y are equal.
a. Equality0
b. Thing
c. Undefined
d. Undefined

31. In mathematics, the additive inverse, or _____ of a number n is the number that, when added to n, yields zero. The additive inverse of n is denoted −n. For example, 7 is −7, because 7 + (−7) = 0, and the additive inverse of −0.3 is 0.3, because −0.3 + 0.3 = 0.
a. Thing
b. Opposite0
c. Undefined
d. Undefined

32. In mathematics, the _____ of a number n is the number that, when added to n, yields zero. The _____ of n is denoted −n. For example, 7 is −7, because 7 + (−7) = 0, and the _____ of −0.3 is 0.3, because −0.3 + 0.3 = 0.
a. Thing
b. Additive inverse0
c. Undefined
d. Undefined

33. In plane geometry, a _____ is a polygon with four equal sides, four right angles, and parallel opposite sides. In algebra, the _____ of a number is that number multiplied by itself.
a. Thing
b. Square0
c. Undefined
d. Undefined

34. In mathematics the _____ refers to the identity: $a^2 - b^2 = (a+b)(a-b)$
a. Difference of two squares0
b. Thing
c. Undefined
d. Undefined

35. In mathematics, the _____ divisor of two non-zero integers, is the largest positive integer that divides both numbers without remainder.
a. Greatest common0
b. Thing
c. Undefined
d. Undefined

36. In Math the greates common divisor sometimes known as the _____ of two non- zero integers.
a. Thing
b. Greatest common factor0
c. Undefined
d. Undefined

37. In mathematics, an _____, mean, or central tendency of a data set refers to a measure of the "middle" or "expected" value of the data set.
a. Average0
b. Concept
c. Undefined
d. Undefined

Chapter 9. Rational Expressions

38. The _____ of measurement are a globally standardized and modernized form of the metric system.
    a. Units0
    b. Thing
    c. Undefined
    d. Undefined

39. In mathematics, a _____ can mean either an element of the set {1, 2, 3, ...} (i.e the positive integers or the counting numbers) or an element of the set {0, 1, 2, 3, ...} (i.e. the non-negative integers).
    a. Thing
    b. Natural number0
    c. Undefined
    d. Undefined

40. _____ is the study of error, particularly in the fields of applied mathematics, applied linguistics, statistics, and numerical analysis.
    a. Error analysis0
    b. Thing
    c. Undefined
    d. Undefined

41. In mathematics, _____ is an elementary arithmetic operation. When one of the numbers is a whole number, _____ is the repeated sum of the other number.
    a. Multiplication0
    b. Thing
    c. Undefined
    d. Undefined

42. _____ or arithmetics is the oldest and most elementary branch of mathematics, used by almost everyone, for tasks ranging from simple daily counting to advanced science and business calculations.
    a. Arithmetic0
    b. Thing
    c. Undefined
    d. Undefined

43. A _____ was a citizen of Babylonia, named for its capital city, Babylon, which was an ancient state in the south part of Mesopotamia (in modern Iraq), combining the territories of Sumer and Akkad.
    a. Babylonian0
    b. Place
    c. Undefined
    d. Undefined

44. A _____ is one of the basic shapes of geometry: a polygon with three vertices and three sides which are straight line segments.
    a. Thing
    b. Triangle0
    c. Undefined
    d. Undefined

45. In mathematics, a _____ is an n-tuple with n being 3.
    a. Thing
    b. Triple0
    c. Undefined
    d. Undefined

46. _____ has one 90° internal angle a right angle.
    a. Thing
    b. Right triangle0
    c. Undefined
    d. Undefined

47. In elementary algebra, a _____ is a polynomial with two terms: the sum of two monomials. It is the simplest kind of polynomial except for a monomial.

Chapter 9. Rational Expressions

a. Thing
c. Undefined
b. Binomial0
d. Undefined

48. In mathematics, the multiplicative inverse of a number x, denoted 1/x or x^{-1}, is the number which, when multiplied by x, yields 1. The multiplicative inverse of x is also called the _____ of x.
   a. Thing
   c. Undefined
   b. Reciprocal0
   d. Undefined

49. _____ is a payment made by a company to its shareholders
   a. Dividend0
   c. Undefined
   b. Thing
   d. Undefined

50. In mathematics, a _____ of an integer n, also called a factor of n, is an integer which evenly divides n without leaving a remainder.
   a. Thing
   c. Undefined
   b. Divisor0
   d. Undefined

51. In mathematics, _____ expressions is used to reduce the expression into the lowest possible term.
   a. Simplifying0
   c. Undefined
   b. Thing
   d. Undefined

52. In abstract algebra, _____ consists of sets with binary operations that satisfy certain axioms.
   a. Thing
   c. Undefined
   b. Grouping0
   d. Undefined

53. _____ are objects, characters, or other concrete representations of ideas, concepts, or other abstractions.
   a. Symbols0
   c. Undefined
   b. Thing
   d. Undefined

54. In arithmetic and algebra, when a number or expression is both preceded and followed by a binary operation, an _____ is required for which operation should be applied first.
   a. Order of operations0
   c. Undefined
   b. Thing
   d. Undefined

55. _____ is the calculated approximation of a result which is usable even if input data may be incomplete, uncertain, or noisy.
   a. Estimation0
   c. Undefined
   b. Concept
   d. Undefined

56. In mathematics, a _____ is a number which can be expressed as a ratio of two integers. Non-integer rational numbers (commonly called fractions) are usually written as the vulgar fraction a / b, where b is not zero.
   a. Concept
   c. Undefined
   b. Rational Number0
   d. Undefined

57. _____, either of the curved-bracket punctuation marks that together make a set of _____

Chapter 9. Rational Expressions

    a. Parentheses0
    c. Undefined
    b. Thing
    d. Undefined

58. Equivalence is the condition of being _____ or essentially equal.
    a. Thing
    c. Undefined
    b. Equivalent0
    d. Undefined

59. In mathematics, _____ growth occurs when the growth rate of a function is always proportional to the function's current size.
    a. Thing
    c. Undefined
    b. Exponential0
    d. Undefined

60. In mathematics, _____ is the decomposition of an object into a product of other objects, or factors, which when multiplied together give the original.
    a. Factoring0
    c. Undefined
    b. Thing
    d. Undefined

61. _____ has many meanings, most of which simply .
    a. Thing
    c. Undefined
    b. Power0
    d. Undefined

62. A _____ is a polynomial consisting of three terms; in other words, it is the sum of three monomials.
    a. Trinomial0
    c. Undefined
    b. Thing
    d. Undefined

63. In mathematics, a _____ number (or a _____) is a natural number that has exactly two (distinct) natural number divisors, which are 1 and the _____ number itself.
    a. Thing
    c. Undefined
    b. Prime0
    d. Undefined

64. _____ is a kind of property which exists as magnitude or multitude. It is among the basic classes of things along with quality, substance, change, and relation.
    a. Amount0
    c. Undefined
    b. Thing
    d. Undefined

65. In mathematics and the mathematical sciences, a _____ is a fixed, but possibly unspecified, value. This is in contrast to a variable, which is not fixed.
    a. Constant0
    c. Undefined
    b. Thing
    d. Undefined

66. In geometry, a _____ is defined as a quadrilateral where all four of its angles are right angles.
    a. Thing
    c. Undefined
    b. Rectangle0
    d. Undefined

67. A _____ is a four-sided plane figure that has two sets of opposite parallel sides.

Chapter 9. Rational Expressions

a. Concept
c. Undefined
b. Parallelogram0
d. Undefined

68. _____ is the transport of people on a trip/journey or the process or time involved in a person or object moving from one location to another.
a. Thing
c. Undefined
b. Travel0
d. Undefined

69. The plus and _____ signs are mathematical symbols used to represent the notions of positive and negative as well as the operations of addition and subtraction.
a. Thing
c. Undefined
b. Minus0
d. Undefined

70. Acid _____ ratio measures the ability of a company to use its near cash or quick assets to immediately extinguish its current liabilities.
a. Thing
c. Undefined
b. Test0
d. Undefined

71. In mathematics, a _____ is a constant multiplicative factor of a certain object. The object can be such things as a variable, a vector, a function, etc. For example, the _____ of $9x^2$ is 9.
a. Coefficient0
c. Undefined
b. Thing
d. Undefined

72. The _____ (symbol _____) and the millibar (symbol mbar, also mb) are units of pressure.
a. Thing
c. Undefined
b. Bar0
d. Undefined

73. In mathematics, and in particular in abstract algebra, the _____ is a property of binary operations that generalises the distributive law from elementary algebra.
a. Thing
c. Undefined
b. Distributive property0
d. Undefined

74. A _____ is a quadrilateral, which is defined as a shape with four sides, which has a pair of parallel sides.
a. Thing
c. Undefined
b. Trapezoid0
d. Undefined

75. In mathematics, _____ is a part of the set theoretic notion of function.
a. Thing
c. Undefined
b. Image0
d. Undefined

76. _____ variables are variables other than the independent variable that may bear any effect on the behavior of the subject being studied.
a. Thing
c. Undefined
b. Extraneous0
d. Undefined

77. In mathematics, a _____ is a polynomial equation of the second degree. The general form is $ax^2 + bx + c = 0$.

Chapter 9. Rational Expressions 121

a. Thing
c. Undefined
b. Quadratic equation0
d. Undefined

78. _____ is a notation for writing numbers that is often used by scientists and mathematicians to make it easier to write large and small numbers.
a. Thing
c. Undefined
b. Scientific notation0
d. Undefined

79. In mathematics, an inequality is a statement about the relative size or order of two objects. For example 14 > 10, or 14 is _____ 10.
a. Thing
c. Undefined
b. Greater than0
d. Undefined

80. _____ element of an element x with respect to a binary operation * with identity element e is an element y such that x * y = y * x = e. In particular,
a. Thing
c. Undefined
b. Inverse0
d. Undefined

81. In mathematics and logic, a _____ proof is a way of showing the truth or falsehood of a given statement by a straightforward combination of established facts, usually existing lemmas and theorems, without making any further assumptions.
a. Direct0
c. Undefined
b. Thing
d. Undefined

82. _____ is the relationship between two variables, like a ratio in which the two quantities being compared are different units.
a. Thing
c. Undefined
b. Direct variation0
d. Undefined

83. In common philosophical language, a proposition or _____, is the content of an assertion, that is, it is true-or-false and defined by the meaning of a particular piece of language.
a. Concept
c. Undefined
b. Statement0
d. Undefined

84. In business, _____, _____ cost or _____ expense refers to an ongoing expense of operating a business.
a. Thing
c. Undefined
b. Overhead0
d. Undefined

85. _____ over a given field is a polynomial with coefficients in that field.
a. Thing
c. Undefined
b. Algebraic equation0
d. Undefined

86. The _____ of a solid object is the three-dimensional concept of how much space it occupies, often quantified numerically.

Chapter 9. Rational Expressions

a. Volume0
c. Undefined
b. Thing
d. Undefined

87. _____ is a physical property of a system that underlies the common notions of hot and cold; something that is hotter has the greater _____.
   a. Thing
   b. Temperature0
   c. Undefined
   d. Undefined

88. A _____ is a special kind of ratio, indicating a relationship between two measurements with different units, such as miles to gallons or cents to pounds.
   a. Rate0
   b. Thing
   c. Undefined
   d. Undefined

89. The _____ of a mathematical object is its size: a property by which it can be larger or smaller than other objects of the same kind; in technical terms, an ordering of the class of objects to which it belongs.
   a. Magnitude0
   b. Thing
   c. Undefined
   d. Undefined

90. In chemistry, a _____ is substance made by combining two or more different materials in such a way that no chemical reaction occurs.
   a. Thing
   b. Mixture0
   c. Undefined
   d. Undefined

91. In business, particularly accounting, a _____ is the time intervals that the accounts, statement, payments, or other calculations cover.
   a. Period0
   b. Thing
   c. Undefined
   d. Undefined

92. A _____ is a unit of length, usually used to measure distance, in a number of different systems, including Imperial units, United States customary units and Norwegian/Swedish mil. Its size can vary from system to system, but in each is between 1 and 10 kilometers. In contemporary English contexts _____ refers to either:
   a. Mile0
   b. Thing
   c. Undefined
   d. Undefined

93. _____ is a unit of speed, expressing the number of international miles covered per hour.
   a. Miles per hour0
   b. Thing
   c. Undefined
   d. Undefined

94. _____ is the estimation of a physical quantity such as distance, energy, temperature, or time.
   a. Measurement0
   b. Thing
   c. Undefined
   d. Undefined

95. _____ is the fee paid on borrowed money.
   a. Thing
   b. Interest0
   c. Undefined
   d. Undefined

Chapter 9. Rational Expressions

96. An _____ is the fee paid on borrow money.
    a. Interest rate0
    c. Undefined
    b. Concept
    d. Undefined

97. _____ or investing is a term with several closely-related meanings in business management, finance and economics, related to saving or deferring consumption.
    a. Investment0
    c. Undefined
    b. Thing
    d. Undefined

98. A _____ are accounts maintained by commercial banks, savings and loan associations, credit unions, and mutual savings banks that pay interest but can not be used directly as money by, for example, writing a cheque.
    a. Thing
    c. Undefined
    b. Savings account0
    d. Undefined

99. _____ means in succession or back-to-back
    a. Consecutive0
    c. Undefined
    b. Thing
    d. Undefined

100. In geometry, the _____ of an object is a point in some sense in the middle of the object.
    a. Center0
    c. Undefined
    b. Thing
    d. Undefined

101. In mathematics, a _____ of a number x is a number r such that $r^2 = x$, or in words, a number r whose square (the result of multiplying the number by itself) is x.
    a. Square root0
    c. Undefined
    b. Thing
    d. Undefined

102. A _____ is an object that is attached to a pivot point so that it can swing freely.
    a. Thing
    c. Undefined
    b. Pendulum0
    d. Undefined

103. In mathematics, a _____ of a complex-valued function f is a member x of the domain of f such that f(x) vanishes at x, that is, x : f (x) = 0.
    a. Root0
    c. Undefined
    b. Thing
    d. Undefined

104. _____ are the basic objects of study in graph theory. Informally speaking, a graph is a set of objects called points, nodes, or vertices connected by links called lines or edges.
    a. Graphs0
    c. Undefined
    b. Thing
    d. Undefined

105. In geometry, a _____ (Greek words diairo = divide and metro = measure) of a circle is any straight line segment that passes through the centre and whose endpoints are on the circular boundary, or, in more modern usage, the length of such a line segment. When using the word in the more modern sense, one speaks of the _____ rather than a _____, because all diameters of a circle have the same length. This length is twice the radius. The _____ of a circle is also the longest chord that the circle has.

Chapter 9. Rational Expressions

a. Thing
c. Undefined
b. Diameter0
d. Undefined

106. _____ is electromagnetic radiation with a wavelength that is visible to the eye (visible _____) or, in a technical or scientific context, electromagnetic radiation of any wavelength.
a. Thing
c. Undefined
b. Light0
d. Undefined

107. A _____ is a function that assigns a number to subsets of a given set.
a. Measure0
c. Undefined
b. Thing
d. Undefined

108. A pair of angles are _____ if the sum of their angles is 90°.
a. Concept
c. Undefined
b. Complementary0
d. Undefined

109. A pair of angles is _____ if their respective measures sum to 180 degrees.
a. Supplementary0
c. Undefined
b. Concept
d. Undefined

110. In combinatorial mathematics, a _____ is an un-ordered collection of unique elements.
a. Combination0
c. Undefined
b. Concept
d. Undefined

111. A _____ is a form of collective investment that pools money from many investors and invests their money in stocks, bonds, short-term money market instruments, and/or other securities.
a. Thing
c. Undefined
b. Mutual fund0
d. Undefined

112. _____ finance, in finance, a debt security, issued by Issuer
a. Bond0
c. Undefined
b. Thing
d. Undefined

113. _____ are economic entities that give rise to future economic benefit and is controlled by the entity as a result of past transaction or other events
a. Thing
c. Undefined
b. Asset0
d. Undefined

114. In the most general sense, a _____ is anything that is a hindrance, or puts individuals at a disadvantage.
a. Liability0
c. Undefined
b. Thing
d. Undefined

115. In mathematics, a _____ is a two-dimensional manifold or surface that is perfectly flat.
a. Thing
c. Undefined
b. Plane0
d. Undefined

Chapter 9. Rational Expressions

116. In mathematics, _____ are two-dimensional manifolds or surfaces that are perfectly flat.
 a. Planes0
 b. Thing
 c. Undefined
 d. Undefined

117. _____ is the speed of an aircraft relative to the air.
 a. Airspeed0
 b. Thing
 c. Undefined
 d. Undefined

118. A _____ is a method of using property as security for the payment of a debt.
 a. Thing
 b. Mortgage0
 c. Undefined
 d. Undefined

119. The _____, the average in everyday English, which is also called the arithmetic _____ (and is distinguished from the geometric _____ or harmonic _____). The average is also called the sample _____. The expected value of a random variable, which is also called the population _____.
 a. Mean0
 b. Thing
 c. Undefined
 d. Undefined

120. In mathematics, a matrix can be thought of as each row or _____ being a vector. Hence, a space formed by row vectors or _____ vectors are said to be a row space or a _____ space.
 a. Concept
 b. Column0
 c. Undefined
 d. Undefined

121. _____ is the distance around a given two-dimensional object. As a general rule, the _____ of a polygon can always be calculated by adding all the length of the sides together. So, the formula for triangles is P = a + b + c, where a, b and c stand for each side of it. For quadrilaterals the equation is P = a + b + c + d. For equilateral polygons, P = na, where n is the number of sides and a is the side length.
 a. Perimeter0
 b. Thing
 c. Undefined
 d. Undefined

122. Initial objects are also called _____, and terminal objects are also called final.
 a. Coterminal0
 b. Thing
 c. Undefined
 d. Undefined

123. An _____ is a straight line or curve A to which another curve B approaches closer and closer as one moves along it. As one moves along B, the space between it and the _____ A becomes smaller and smaller, and can in fact be made as small as one could wish by going far enough along. A curve may or may not touch or cross its _____. In fact, the curve may intersect the _____ an infinite number of times.
 a. Asymptote0
 b. Thing
 c. Undefined
 d. Undefined

124. _____ is a method of describing limiting behavior.
 a. Asymptotic0
 b. Thing
 c. Undefined
 d. Undefined

125. In mathematics, the _____ of a coordinate system is the point where the axes of the system intersect.

a. Origin0
b. Thing
c. Undefined
d. Undefined

126. _____ is a straight line or curve A to which another curve B the one being studied approaches closer and closer as one moves along it.
   a. Vertical asymptote0
   b. Thing
   c. Undefined
   d. Undefined

127. In astronomy, geography, geometry and related sciences and contexts, a plane is said to be _____ at a given point if it is locally perpendicular to the gradient of the gravity field, i.e., with the direction of the gravitational force at that point.
   a. Horizontal0
   b. Thing
   c. Undefined
   d. Undefined

Chapter 10. Exponential and Logarithmic Functions

1. _____ or arithmetics (from the Greek word áñéèìùò = number) in common usage is a branch of (or the forerunner of) mathematics which records elementary properties of certain operations on numerals, though in usage by professional mathematicians, it often is treated as a synonym for number theory.
   - a. Arithmetic10
   - b. ADE classification
   - c. Undefined
   - d. Undefined

2. The word _____ can have three meanings: In _____ theory, a _____ is an abstract object consisting of vertices (or nodes) and edges (or arcs) between pairs of vertices. The _____ of a function f : X ¨ Y is the set of all pairs (x,f(x)) The _____ of a relation, a generalisation of the _____ of a function.
   - a. Graph10
   - b. -equivalence
   - c. Undefined
   - d. Undefined

3. A _____ is an undefined term. However, it is often thought of as a series of points. A _____ has one dimension - length. A _____ is either named by a lower case letter or by two points on the _____.
   - a. Line10
   - b. -equivalence
   - c. Undefined
   - d. Undefined

4. A number that does not change in value in a given situation is a _____.
   - a. -equivalence
   - b. Constant10
   - c. Undefined
   - d. Undefined

5. A _____ is the relationship between two quantities. It is expressed as the quotient of two numbers, or as two numbers separated by a colon (pronounced "to"). A number that can be written as a _____ of two integers is a rational number.
   - a. -equivalence
   - b. Ratio10
   - c. Undefined
   - d. Undefined

6. A _____ is a number or variable, or the product or quotient of a number or variable.
   - a. Term10
   - b. -equivalence
   - c. Undefined
   - d. Undefined

7. The answer to subtraction is called the _____.
   - a. -equivalence
   - b. Difference10
   - c. Undefined
   - d. Undefined

8. <U>Factor</U> is any number that multiples to get a product..
   - a. -equivalence
   - b. Factor10
   - c. Undefined
   - d. Undefined

9. A number that is raised to a power, or _____ of an exponential function. This finds common use, for example, in the depiction of numbers, for instance, 10 is the _____ used in the decimal system, whereas 2 is the _____ in the binary numeral system.
   - a. -equivalence
   - b. Base10
   - c. Undefined
   - d. Undefined

10. A <U>function</U> is a relation where every x value has one and only y value.

a. Function10
b. -equivalence
c. Undefined
d. Undefined

11. The very fact that we are measuring objects with respect to some characteristic implies that the objects differ in that characteristic; or stated in another way, that the characteristic can take on a number of different values. These properties or characteristics of an object that can assume two or more different values are referred to as a _____.
   a. Variable10
   b. -equivalence
   c. Undefined
   d. Undefined

12. The _____ indicates how many of the base to multiply together to get the product. When 5 to the third power is 125, then 3 is the _____ and can also be called a power.
   a. ADE classification
   b. Exponent10
   c. Undefined
   d. Undefined

13. An _____ is represented by two expressions that have the same value.
   a. ADE classification
   b. Equation10
   c. Undefined
   d. Undefined

14. An _____ is a variable, constant, or any combination that contains an exponent. Examples are 3^{5}, x^{w}, and $4x^{5}$,
   a. Exponential expression10
   b. ADE classification
   c. Undefined
   d. Undefined

15. An _____ combines numbers, operators, and/or variables but contains no equal or inequality sign.
   a. ADE classification
   b. Expression10
   c. Undefined
   d. Undefined

16. Whenever a number is written in exponential e.pression, the exponent can also be called a power.
   a. -equivalence
   b. Power10
   c. Undefined
   d. Undefined

17. The domain of a graph or equation is the set of all the possible x values.
   a. Domain10
   b. -equivalence
   c. Undefined
   d. Undefined

18. A measure of variability, the _____ is the distance from the lowest to the highest score.
   a. -equivalence
   b. Range10
   c. Undefined
   d. Undefined

19. By _____ we mean collecting observations made upon our environment -- observations, which are the results of measurements using clocks, balances, measuring rods, counting operations, or other objectively defined measuring instruments or procedures. _____ may mean simply counting the number of times a particular property occurs.
   a. Data10
   b. -equivalence
   c. Undefined
   d. Undefined

Chapter 10. Exponential and Logarithmic Functions

20. _____ are intuitively defined as numbers that are in one-to-one correspondence with the points on an infinite line—the number line. The term "real number" is a retronym coined in response to "imaginary number" _____ may be rational or irrational; algebraic or transcendental; and positive, negative, or zero _____ measure continuous quantities. They may in theory be expressed by decimal fractions that have an infinite sequence of digits to the right of the decimal point; these are often (mis-)represented in the same form as 324.823211247... (where the three dots express that there would still be more digits to come, no matter how many more might be added at the end).
    a. -equivalence
    b. Real numbers10
    c. Undefined
    d. Undefined

21. A _____ is a well-defined collection of objects considered as a whole.
    a. Set10
    b. -equivalence
    c. Undefined
    d. Undefined

22. The amount of money paid for borrowing or investing money is called the <U>interest</U>. There are two main kinds of _____ called simple _____ and compound _____.
    a. ADE classification
    b. Interest10
    c. Undefined
    d. Undefined

23. When something occurs once a year it is said to occur <U>annually.</U>
    a. Annually10
    b. ADE classification
    c. Undefined
    d. Undefined

24. The amount of money borrowed or invested is called the <U>principal.</U>
    a. -equivalence
    b. Principal10
    c. Undefined
    d. Undefined

25. There are properties of objects that do assume one and only value, and we refer to these characteristics as _____. _____, then, are the invariables that differentiate one class of objects from another.
    a. Constants10
    b. -equivalence
    c. Undefined
    d. Undefined

26. When a number in decimal form does not repeat nor terminate, it is an _____. Pi and the square root of 7 are example s of an _____.
    a. ADE classification
    b. Irrational number10
    c. Undefined
    d. Undefined

27. _____, or less commonly, denary, usually refers to the base 10 numeral system.
    a. -equivalence
    b. Decimal10
    c. Undefined
    d. Undefined

28. _____ consist of the positive natural numbers (1, 2, 3, ...), their negatives (−1, −2, −3, ...) and the number zero.
    a. ADE classification
    b. Integers10
    c. Undefined
    d. Undefined

Chapter 10. Exponential and Logarithmic Functions

29. An _____ is an indication of the value of an unknown quantity based on observed data. More formally, an _____ is the particular value of an estimator that is obtained from a particular sample of data and used to indicate the value of a parameter.
    a. ADE classification
    b. Estimate10
    c. Undefined
    d. Undefined

30. _____ is the process by which sample data are used to indicate the value of an unknown quantity in a population.
    a. Estimation10
    b. ADE classification
    c. Undefined
    d. Undefined

31. A _____ goes from left to right or from East to West.
    a. -equivalence
    b. Horizontal line10
    c. Undefined
    d. Undefined

32. A _____ is an undefined term. We usually represent this by a dot, but a _____ actually has no dimension. A capital letter names any _____.
    a. -equivalence
    b. Point10
    c. Undefined
    d. Undefined

33. The _____ refers to the amount of change in Y for a 1 unit change in X or is the ratio of the rise over the run; or in-other-words, the rate of change in the predicted value as a function of a change in the predictor variable.
    a. -equivalence
    b. Slope10
    c. Undefined
    d. Undefined

34. The _____ is t the point where a graph intersects the y-axis and is found by setting x = 0 and then sovling for the y-value.
    a. Y-intercept10
    b. -equivalence
    c. Undefined
    d. Undefined

35. In a large distribution of data it is often easier to understand the data if it is grouped into intervals where each _____ can contain more than one data value. Distributions are often reduced to 10 to 20 intervals.
    a. ADE classification
    b. Interval10
    c. Undefined
    d. Undefined

36. When a number is written with an exponent this number will be in _____.
    a. ADE classification
    b. Exponential form10
    c. Undefined
    d. Undefined

37. Whenever you divide by zero the answer is _____.
    a. Undefined10
    b. ADE classification
    c. Undefined
    d. Undefined

38. The _____ is the point where a graph intersects the x-axis and is found by letting y = 0 and then solving for the x-value.

Chapter 10. Exponential and Logarithmic Functions

a. X-intercept10
b. -equivalence
c. Undefined
d. Undefined

39. The combination of a particular row and column; the set of observations obtained under identical treatment conditions is simply a _____.
   a. Cell10
   b. -equivalence
   c. Undefined
   d. Undefined

40. A _____, also referred to as a universe, is any well-defined collection of things. By well-defined we mean that the members of the _____ are spelled out, or an unequivocal statement is made as to which things belong in it and which do not.
   a. -equivalence
   b. Population10
   c. Undefined
   d. Undefined

41. In a proportion the "middle" values are often referred to as the <U>means.</U>
   a. -equivalence
   b. Means10
   c. Undefined
   d. Undefined

42. The most important measure of central tendency, and one of the basic building blocks of all statistical analysis, is the arithmetic _____. It is simply the sum of all the set of values divided by the number of values involved. It can also be called the average.
   a. -equivalence
   b. Mean10
   c. Undefined
   d. Undefined

43. Any number that is divisible by 2 is an <U>even</U> number.
   a. ADE classification
   b. Even10
   c. Undefined
   d. Undefined

44. The first grouping symbol used are called <U>parentheses</U> ( ).
   a. Parentheses10
   b. -equivalence
   c. Undefined
   d. Undefined

45. An _____ is an action applied to numbers or other entities to produce a well-defined result.
   a. Operation10
   b. ADE classification
   c. Undefined
   d. Undefined

46. A <U>product i</U>s the answer in multiplication, or an expression that identifies factors to be multiplied
   a. -equivalence
   b. Product10
   c. Undefined
   d. Undefined

47. A _____ is the end result of a division problem. For example, in the problem 6 ÷ 3, the _____ would be 2, while 6 would be called the dividend, and 3 the divisor
   a. -equivalence
   b. Quotient10
   c. Undefined
   d. Undefined

48. _____ are characteristics or properties of an object that can take on one or more different values.

Chapter 10. Exponential and Logarithmic Functions

    a. -equivalence   b. Variables10
    c. Undefined   d. Undefined

49. A _____ is a multiplicative factor of a certain object such as a variable (for example, the coefficients of a polynomial), a basis vector, a basis function and so on. Usually, the objects and the coefficients are indexed in the same way, leading to expressions such as a1x1 + a2x2 + a3x3 + ... where an is the _____ of the variable xn for each n = 1, 2, 3, ...
    a. -equivalence   b. Coefficient10
    c. Undefined   d. Undefined

50. _____ is the property of multiplication over addition which demonstrates that for all numbers a,b,c; a(b+c)=ab+ac, and ab+ac=a(b+c).
    a. Distributive property10   b. -equivalence
    c. Undefined   d. Undefined

51. When the greatest common factor becomes one factor of a product, this is when to <U>factor out </U>a common factor.
    a. -equivalence   b. Factor out10
    c. Undefined   d. Undefined

52. A _____ contains at least one squared term.
    a. -equivalence   b. Quadratic10
    c. Undefined   d. Undefined

53. _____ occur when each term contains the very same variable to the same power. 3x and -5x are examples of _____.
    a. Like Terms10   b. -equivalence
    c. Undefined   d. Undefined

54. A _____ is written in standard form as ax^3+ bx + c = 0. In general, a _____ must contain a squared term.
    a. Quadratic equation10   b. -equivalence
    c. Undefined   d. Undefined

55. A _____ is a concrete example of an item or a specification against which all others may be measured. For example, there are "primary standards" for length, mass (see Kilogram standard), and other units of measure, kept by laboratories and standards organizations.
    a. Standard10   b. -equivalence
    c. Undefined   d. Undefined

56. At times we must contend with variables that assume a large number of values. In this case it is typical to create _____ of values of the variable and then make a frequency tally of the number of observations falling within each interval. As is the case with any data reduction technique, detail is lost.
    a. Intervals10   b. ADE classification
    c. Undefined   d. Undefined

Chapter 10. Exponential and Logarithmic Functions

57. An event that occurs every 3 months is said to occur _____.
   a. -equivalence
   b. Quarterly10
   c. Undefined
   d. Undefined

58. A _____ is a scheme for the numerical representation of the values of a variable. The interpretation we place upon the numbers of the _____, rather than the numbers themselves, makes the _____ useful. The most common scales are nominal, ordinal, interval
   a. Scale10
   b. -equivalence
   c. Undefined
   d. Undefined

59. _____ is the result of assigning numbers to objects to abstractly represent the objects or characteristics of the objects.
   a. -equivalence
   b. Measurement10
   c. Undefined
   d. Undefined

60. Any time one number is on the left side of another number on a number line, the first number is _____ the second number. The symbol for this is <.
   a. Less than10
   b. -equivalence
   c. Undefined
   d. Undefined

61. _____ is the change in x between two points
   a. -equivalence
   b. Run10
   c. Undefined
   d. Undefined

62. An _____ is any process or study, which results in the collection of data, the outcome of which is unknown. In statistics, the term is usually restricted to situations in which the researcher has control over some of the conditions under which the _____ takes place.
   a. ADE classification
   b. Experiment10
   c. Undefined
   d. Undefined

Chapter 11. A Preview of College Algebra

1. _____ is a branch of mathematics which studies structure and quantity. It may be roughly characterized as a generalization and abstraction of arithmetic, in which operations are performed on symbols rather than numbers. It includes elementary _____, taught to high school students, as well as abstract _____ which covers such structures as groups, rings and fields. Along with geometry and analysis, it is one of the three principal branches of mathematics.
   a. ADE classification
   b. Algebra11
   c. Undefined
   d. Undefined

2. A <U>function</U> is a relation where every x value has one and only y value.
   a. -equivalence
   b. Function11
   c. Undefined
   d. Undefined

3. A number that does not change in value in a given situation is a _____.
   a. Constant11
   b. -equivalence
   c. Undefined
   d. Undefined

4. The word _____ can have three meanings: In _____ theory, a _____ is an abstract object consisting of vertices (or nodes) and edges (or arcs) between pairs of vertices. The _____ of a function f : X ¨ Y is the set of all pairs (x,f(x)) The _____ of a relation, a generalisation of the _____ of a function.
   a. -equivalence
   b. Graph11
   c. Undefined
   d. Undefined

5. A _____ goes from left to right or from East to West.
   a. Horizontal line11
   b. -equivalence
   c. Undefined
   d. Undefined

6. A _____ is an undefined term. However, it is often thought of as a series of points. A _____ has one dimension - length. A _____ is either named by a lower case letter or by two points on the _____.
   a. -equivalence
   b. Line11
   c. Undefined
   d. Undefined

7. The graph of a quadrataic equation is a symmetric curve called a <U>parabola.</U>
   a. Parabola11
   b. -equivalence
   c. Undefined
   d. Undefined

8. A <U>vertex</U> is the point that occurs whenever two lines, line segments, or rays meet. The _____ of an angle is very important.
   a. Vertex11
   b. -equivalence
   c. Undefined
   d. Undefined

9. The <U>domain</U> of a graph or equation is the set of all the possible x values.
   a. Domain11
   b. -equivalence
   c. Undefined
   d. Undefined

10. _____ are intuitively defined as numbers that are in one-to-one correspondence with the points on an infinite line—the number line. The term "real number" is a retronym coined in response to "imaginary number" _____ may be rational or irrational; algebraic or transcendental; and positive, negative, or zero _____ measure continuous quantities. They may in theory be expressed by decimal fractions that have an infinite sequence of digits to the right of the decimal point; these are often (mis-)represented in the same form as 324.823211247... (where the three dots express that there would still be more digits to come, no matter how many more might be added at the end).

a. Real numbers11
b. -equivalence
c. Undefined
d. Undefined

11. A _____ is a well-defined collection of objects considered as a whole.

a. Set11
b. -equivalence
c. Undefined
d. Undefined

12. A _____ of an integer n, also called a factor of n, is an integer which evenly divides n without leaving a remainder.

a. Divisor11
b. -equivalence
c. Undefined
d. Undefined

13. An _____ combines numbers, operators, and/or variables but contains no equal or inequality sign.

a. Expression11
b. ADE classification
c. Undefined
d. Undefined

14. The answer to subtraction is called the _____.

a. Difference11
b. -equivalence
c. Undefined
d. Undefined

15. The bottom part of any fraction represents the number of pieces in one whole unit. This bottom part is called the _____.

a. -equivalence
b. Denominator11
c. Undefined
d. Undefined

16. In a proportion the "middle" values are often referred to as the <U>means.</U>

a. -equivalence
b. Means11
c. Undefined
d. Undefined

17. _____ is a quick way of adding identical numbers. For example, the sum 7 + 7 + 7 can be found by multiplying 3 times 7. This model is reflected in the use of the word times as a synonym for multiplied by. The resuult of multiplying numbers is called a product. The numbers being multiplied are called factors.

a. -equivalence
b. Multiplication11
c. Undefined
d. Undefined

18. <U>Length</U> measure how long something is.

a. -equivalence
b. Length11
c. Undefined
d. Undefined

19. A quadrilateral with 4 equal sides and all right angles is called a _____.

Chapter 11. A Preview of College Algebra

    a. Square11
    c. Undefined
    b. -equivalence
    d. Undefined

20. An _____ is represented by two expressions that have the same value.
    a. Equation11
    b. ADE classification
    c. Undefined
    d. Undefined

21. _____ is the distance around a polygon. It can be found by adding the lengths of all sides.
    a. -equivalence
    b. Perimeter11
    c. Undefined
    d. Undefined

22. Addition (or summation) is one of the basic operations of arithmetic. In its simplest form, addition combines two numbers, the augend and addend, into a single number, the _____. Adding more numbers can be viewed as repeated addition. (Repeated addition of the number one is the most basic form of counting.) By extension, the addition of zero numbers, one number, or infinitely many numbers can be defined.
    a. -equivalence
    b. Sum11
    c. Undefined
    d. Undefined

23. A _____ is an undefined term. We can think of it as a series of lines having 2 dimensions, width and length.
    a. Plane11
    b. -equivalence
    c. Undefined
    d. Undefined

24. _____ or arithmetics (from the Greek word áñéèìùò = number) in common usage is a branch of (or the forerunner of) mathematics which records elementary properties of certain operations on numerals, though in usage by professional mathematicians, it often is treated as a synonym for number theory.
    a. ADE classification
    b. Arithmetic11
    c. Undefined
    d. Undefined

25. _____ refer to any data source, whether individuals, physical or biological things, geographic locations, time periods, or events; that is, anything upon which observations can be made.
    a. ADE classification
    b. Objects11
    c. Undefined
    d. Undefined

26. By _____ we mean collecting observations made upon our environment -- observations, which are the results of measurements using clocks, balances, measuring rods, counting operations, or other objectively defined measuring instruments or procedures. _____ may mean simply counting the number of times a particular property occurs.
    a. -equivalence
    b. Data11
    c. Undefined
    d. Undefined

27. A _____ is a number or variable, or the product or quotient of a number or variable.
    a. Term11
    b. -equivalence
    c. Undefined
    d. Undefined

28. A _____ is the relationship between two quantities. It is expressed as the quotient of two numbers, or as two numbers separated by a colon (pronounced "to"). A number that can be written as a _____ of two integers is a rational number.

a. -equivalence b. Ratio11
c. Undefined d. Undefined

29. Horizontal axis of display containing the trailing digits is called _____.
a. -equivalence b. Leaves11
c. Undefined d. Undefined

30. An event that occurs every 3 months is said to occur _____.
a. Quarterly11 b. -equivalence
c. Undefined d. Undefined

31. A _____ contains at least one squared term.
a. -equivalence b. Quadratic11
c. Undefined d. Undefined

32. In general, the word _____ usually is used as a prefix for other words. _____ literally means under. When we see x_[, we refer to this as x _____ 1.
a. Sub11 b. -equivalence
c. Undefined d. Undefined

33. The <U>index</U> of a radical expression stands for the root that needs to be taken. It appears as the smaller number at the upper left of the radical symbol.
a. ADE classification b. Index11
c. Undefined d. Undefined

34. The very fact that we are measuring objects with respect to some characteristic implies that the objects differ in that characteristic; or stated in another way, that the characteristic can take on a number of different values. These properties or characteristics of an object that can assume two or more different values are referred to as a _____.
a. Variable11 b. -equivalence
c. Undefined d. Undefined

35. _____ consist of the positive natural numbers (1, 2, 3, ...), their negatives (−1, −2, −3, ...) and the number zero.
a. ADE classification b. Integers11
c. Undefined d. Undefined

36. When terms have the same exact variables to the same exact exponents, they are called like terms or <U>similar terms</U>.
a. -equivalence b. Similar terms11
c. Undefined d. Undefined

37. An _____ is an action applied to numbers or other entities to produce a well-defined result.
a. ADE classification b. Operation11
c. Undefined d. Undefined

38. A piece of a circle is called an _____.

a. ADE classification
c. Undefined
b. Arc11
d. Undefined

39. One of the grouping symbols used are called _____ [ ].
   a. -equivalence
   b. Brackets11
   c. Undefined
   d. Undefined

40. There are properties of objects that do assume one and only value, and we refer to these characteristics as _____. _____, then, are the invariables that differentiate one class of objects from another.
   a. -equivalence
   b. Constants11
   c. Undefined
   d. Undefined

41. An _____ is two numbers, where the first number represents a value on the horizontal axis, and the second number represents a value on the vertical axis, such as (x,y).
   a. ADE classification
   b. Ordered pair11
   c. Undefined
   d. Undefined

42. When the parts of a fraction have no common factors, the fraction is said to be _____ to lowest terms.
   a. -equivalence
   b. Reduced11
   c. Undefined
   d. Undefined

43. _____ (or summation) is one of the basic operations of arithmetic. In its simplest form, _____ combines two numbers, the augend and addend, into a single number, the sum.
   a. ADE classification
   b. Addition11
   c. Undefined
   d. Undefined

44. An <U>inconsistent system </U>has no solution.
   a. ADE classification
   b. Inconsistent system11
   c. Undefined
   d. Undefined

45. _____ are characteristics or properties of an object that can take on one or more different values.
   a. Variables11
   b. -equivalence
   c. Undefined
   d. Undefined

46. A _____ is an equation which is constructed by equating two linear functions of which the highest exponent is one.
   a. Linear equation11
   b. -equivalence
   c. Undefined
   d. Undefined

47. When 2 or more equations are considered as a group, this creates a <U>system of equations.</U>
   a. System of equations11
   b. -equivalence
   c. Undefined
   d. Undefined

48. A _____ is an undefined term. We usually represent this by a dot, but a _____ actually has no dimension. A capital letter names any _____.

Chapter 11. A Preview of College Algebra

a. -equivalence
c. Undefined
b. Point11
d. Undefined

49. A <U>dependent system </U>of equations has an infinite number of solutions.
    a. -equivalence
    c. Undefined
    b. Dependent system11
    d. Undefined

50. _____ means to multiply by 2.
    a. -equivalence
    c. Undefined
    b. Twice11
    d. Undefined

51. Any polygon that has 3 sides is called a _____.
    a. Triangle11
    c. Undefined
    b. -equivalence
    d. Undefined

52. Any time one number is on the left side of another number on a number line, the first number is _____ the second number. The symbol for this is <.
    a. -equivalence
    c. Undefined
    b. Less than11
    d. Undefined

53. An _____ is composed of two rays that have a common endpoint, called the vertex. Each _____ is named by a lower case letter or by one point from each ray and the vertex inbetween. _____ a might be the same _____ as _____ ABC.
    a. ADE classification
    c. Undefined
    b. Angle11
    d. Undefined

54. The <U>distance formula</U> is that rate times time equals distance or d = rt.
    a. Distance formula11
    c. Undefined
    b. -equivalence
    d. Undefined

55. The _____ is often confused with the median. The Median is a statistic for the distribution whereas the _____ provides a statistic for an interval; it is the center of the interval; the arithmetic average of the upper and lower limits.
    a. -equivalence
    c. Undefined
    b. Midpoint11
    d. Undefined

56. One major objective of statistical analysis is the identification of associations or _____ that exist between and among sets of observations. In other words, does knowledge about about one set of data allow us to infer or predict characteristics about another set or sets of data.
    a. -equivalence
    c. Undefined
    b. Relationships11
    d. Undefined

57. A _____ is a series of points the same distance from a given point, called the center.
    a. -equivalence
    c. Undefined
    b. Circle11
    d. Undefined

Chapter 11. A Preview of College Algebra

58. The _____ of a circle is a chord that goes through the center.
    a. Diameter11
    c. Undefined
    b. -equivalence
    d. Undefined

59. A _____ is a piece of a line. The _____ has definite length and is named by the two endpoints.
    a. -equivalence
    c. Undefined
    b. Line segment11
    d. Undefined

60. The _____ of a circle is the distance from the center to the circle.
    a. -equivalence
    c. Undefined
    b. Radius11
    d. Undefined

61. A _____ is a concrete example of an item or a specification against which all others may be measured. For example, there are "primary standards" for length, mass (see Kilogram standard), and other units of measure, kept by laboratories and standards organizations.
    a. -equivalence
    c. Undefined
    b. Standard11
    d. Undefined

62. An _____ is one of the number lines found on the rectangular coordinate system. The x asis is the horizontal number line while the y _____ is the vertical number line.
    a. ADE classification
    c. Undefined
    b. Axis11
    d. Undefined

63. The point of intersection of the horizontal and vertical axes in the rectangular coordinate plane is the _____. It is is expressed as the ordered pair (0,0).
    a. ADE classification
    c. Undefined
    b. Origin11
    d. Undefined

64. A quadrilateral with opposite sides equal and parallel and containing all right angles is called a _____.
    a. Rectangle11
    c. Undefined
    b. -equivalence
    d. Undefined

65. A number that is raised to a power, or _____ of an exponential function. This finds common use, for example, in the depiction of numbers, for instance, 10 is the _____ used in the decimal system, whereas 2 is the _____ in the binary numeral system.
    a. Base11
    c. Undefined
    b. -equivalence
    d. Undefined

66. <U>Weight</U> measures how heavy or light something is.
    a. Weight11
    c. Undefined
    b. -equivalence
    d. Undefined

ANSWER KEY

Chapter 1

1. b	2. a	3. a	4. a	5. a	6. a	7. a	8. a	9. a	10. a
11. a	12. b	13. b	14. a	15. b	16. a	17. a	18. a	19. a	20. a
21. b	22. b	23. a	24. a	25. a	26. b	27. b	28. a	29. b	30. a
31. a	32. b	33. a	34. b	35. b	36. a	37. a	38. a	39. b	40. b
41. a	42. a	43. b	44. a	45. a	46. a	47. a	48. b	49. a	50. a
51. b	52. b	53. b	54. b	55. b	56. a	57. a	58. a	59. b	60. b
61. a	62. b	63. b	64. b	65. b	66. a	67. b	68. a	69. b	70. a
71. b	72. b	73. b	74. b	75. b	76. b	77. b	78. a	79. a	80. b
81. a	82. b	83. a	84. a	85. b	86. a	87. a	88. a	89. b	90. b
91. a	92. b	93. b	94. a	95. a	96. a	97. b	98. a	99. a	100. a
101. b	102. a	103. b	104. b	105. a	106. b	107. b	108. b	109. a	110. b
111. b	112. b	113. a	114. b	115. b	116. a	117. b	118. b	119. b	120. b
121. a	122. a	123. a	124. b	125. a	126. a	127. b	128. a	129. b	130. a
131. a	132. b	133. b	134. b	135. a	136. b	137. a	138. b	139. b	140. b
141. a	142. a	143. a	144. b	145. b	146. b	147. a	148. b	149. b	150. a
151. a	152. b	153. a	154. b	155. a	156. a	157. b	158. a	159. a	160. b
161. b	162. a	163. b	164. a	165. a	166. b	167. b	168. a	169. b	170. a
171. a	172. a								

Chapter 2

1. a	2. b	3. b	4. a	5. b	6. b	7. b	8. a	9. a	10. b
11. b	12. a	13. a	14. b	15. b	16. a	17. b	18. a	19. b	20. b
21. b	22. a	23. b	24. a	25. a	26. b	27. b	28. a	29. a	30. a
31. a	32. a	33. a	34. a	35. a	36. a	37. b	38. a	39. b	40. b
41. b	42. a	43. a	44. b	45. b	46. b	47. a	48. a	49. a	50. b
51. a	52. b	53. b	54. a	55. b	56. b	57. a	58. b	59. a	60. a
61. a	62. b	63. b	64. a	65. b	66. a	67. b	68. a	69. b	70. a
71. a	72. b	73. b	74. b	75. a	76. a	77. b	78. b	79. a	80. b
81. a	82. b	83. b	84. a	85. a	86. a	87. b	88. a	89. b	90. b
91. b	92. a	93. b	94. a	95. a	96. b	97. a	98. a	99. b	100. b
101. a	102. b	103. b	104. b	105. a	106. a	107. b	108. b	109. b	110. b
111. a	112. a	113. b	114. b	115. b	116. b	117. b	118. a	119. b	120. a
121. b	122. b	123. a	124. a	125. a					

Chapter 3

1. b	2. b	3. b	4. b	5. b	6. a	7. a	8. a	9. a	10. b
11. b	12. a	13. a	14. a	15. b	16. b	17. b	18. a	19. a	20. a
21. b	22. a	23. a	24. a	25. a	26. b	27. b	28. b	29. a	30. a
31. b	32. a	33. b	34. b	35. b	36. a	37. a	38. a	39. a	40. b
41. a	42. a	43. a	44. b	45. b	46. b	47. a	48. b	49. b	50. a
51. b	52. b	53. a	54. a	55. a	56. b	57. b	58. a	59. b	60. b
61. b	62. a	63. b	64. a	65. a	66. b	67. b	68. b	69. b	70. a
71. a	72. b	73. a	74. b	75. a	76. a	77. b	78. b	79. a	80. a
81. a	82. a	83. b	84. b	85. a	86. a	87. b	88. a	89. a	90. a
91. b	92. b	93. b	94. a	95. b	96. b	97. b	98. a	99. a	100. a
101. a	102. a	103. a	104. b	105. b	106. b	107. a	108. a	109. b	110. a
111. a	112. a	113. b	114. a	115. b	116. a	117. b	118. b	119. b	120. a

Chapter 4

1. a	2. b	3. a	4. b	5. a	6. a	7. a	8. b	9. a	10. b
11. b	12. b	13. b	14. a	15. b	16. a	17. a	18. b	19. b	20. a
21. b	22. b	23. a	24. b	25. a	26. a	27. b	28. b	29. a	30. a
31. b	32. a	33. a	34. a	35. b	36. b	37. b	38. b	39. a	40. a
41. b	42. b	43. a	44. a	45. b	46. b	47. b	48. a	49. a	50. b
51. b	52. b	53. b	54. b	55. a	56. a	57. a	58. a	59. b	60. a
61. a	62. a	63. b	64. b	65. b	66. a	67. a	68. b	69. a	70. b
71. b	72. b	73. b	74. b	75. a	76. a	77. b	78. a	79. a	80. a
81. b	82. b	83. b							

Chapter 5

1. b	2. a	3. a	4. b	5. a	6. a	7. b	8. b	9. a	10. a
11. a	12. a	13. b	14. a	15. a	16. a	17. a	18. b	19. a	20. a
21. a	22. a	23. b	24. b	25. b	26. b	27. b	28. b	29. a	30. a
31. b	32. b	33. a	34. b	35. a	36. a	37. a	38. a	39. b	40. a
41. b	42. b	43. a	44. b	45. b	46. a	47. b	48. a	49. a	50. b
51. a	52. a	53. b	54. b	55. b	56. b	57. b	58. a	59. b	60. a
61. a	62. b	63. a	64. b	65. a	66. b	67. a	68. b	69. a	70. a
71. b	72. b	73. b	74. a	75. a	76. b	77. a	78. a	79. b	80. b
81. a	82. b	83. a	84. b	85. a	86. b	87. b	88. a	89. b	90. b
91. b	92. a	93. a	94. b	95. a	96. b	97. a	98. a	99. a	100. b
101. b	102. b	103. a	104. a	105. b	106. a	107. b	108. a	109. a	110. a
111. b	112. a	113. b	114. b	115. b	116. a	117. b	118. a	119. b	120. b
121. b	122. a	123. b	124. a	125. a	126. a	127. a	128. a	129. b	130. b
131. a	132. a	133. b	134. a	135. b	136. a	137. b	138. b	139. b	140. a
141. a	142. a	143. b	144. a	145. b	146. b	147. b	148. a	149. b	

ANSWER KEY

Chapter 6

1. b	2. a	3. b	4. a	5. b	6. a	7. a	8. b	9. a	10. a
11. b	12. a	13. b	14. a	15. b	16. a	17. b	18. b	19. b	20. b
21. b	22. b	23. a	24. b	25. a	26. b	27. a	28. b	29. a	30. a
31. a	32. a	33. b	34. a	35. a	36. b	37. a	38. b	39. b	40. a
41. b	42. b	43. b	44. b	45. b	46. a	47. a	48. b	49. a	50. a
51. b	52. a	53. b	54. b	55. a	56. a	57. b	58. b	59. a	60. a
61. b	62. a	63. a	64. a	65. b	66. a	67. a	68. a	69. a	70. b
71. b	72. a	73. b	74. b	75. a	76. b	77. b	78. b	79. a	80. b
81. a	82. a	83. b	84. a	85. b	86. b	87. b	88. a	89. a	90. a
91. b	92. b	93. a	94. b	95. a	96. a	97. a	98. a	99. b	100. b
101. b	102. b	103. b	104. b	105. a	106. b	107. b	108. a	109. b	110. b
111. b	112. a	113. a	114. b	115. a	116. b	117. a	118. b	119. b	120. a
121. b	122. b	123. a	124. b	125. a	126. a	127. a	128. a		

Chapter 7

1. b	2. b	3. a	4. b	5. b	6. b	7. a	8. a	9. a	10. a
11. b	12. a	13. b	14. a	15. a	16. a	17. a	18. a	19. a	20. a
21. a	22. a	23. a	24. b	25. a	26. a	27. a	28. b	29. b	30. b
31. b	32. a	33. a	34. a	35. a	36. b	37. a	38. b	39. a	40. a
41. a	42. b	43. a	44. a	45. b	46. b	47. b	48. a	49. a	50. a
51. b	52. b	53. b	54. a	55. a	56. b	57. a	58. b	59. b	60. b
61. b	62. a	63. b	64. a	65. a	66. b	67. b	68. b		

Chapter 8

1. b	2. b	3. b	4. b	5. b	6. b	7. b	8. a	9. a	10. a
11. b	12. b	13. a	14. a	15. a	16. a	17. b	18. b	19. b	20. a
21. a	22. b	23. b	24. a	25. a	26. a	27. a	28. a	29. a	30. b
31. a	32. b	33. a	34. b	35. a	36. a	37. b	38. a	39. b	40. a
41. a	42. b	43. a	44. b	45. a	46. a	47. b	48. a	49. a	50. a
51. a	52. b	53. a	54. b	55. a	56. a	57. a	58. a	59. a	60. a
61. b	62. a	63. b	64. b	65. a	66. a	67. b	68. b	69. b	70. b
71. a	72. a	73. a	74. a	75. a	76. b	77. b	78. b	79. a	80. a
81. b	82. a	83. b	84. a	85. a	86. b	87. b	88. a	89. a	90. b
91. a	92. b	93. b	94. b	95. b	96. a	97. b	98. b	99. b	100. a
101. a	102. a	103. a	104. a	105. b	106. a	107. b	108. b	109. b	110. a
111. b	112. a	113. b	114. b	115. a	116. a	117. b	118. a	119. a	120. a
121. b	122. b	123. a	124. b	125. b	126. b	127. b	128. a	129. b	130. b
131. a	132. b	133. b	134. b	135. b	136. b	137. a	138. b	139. a	140. b
141. b	142. a	143. b	144. a	145. b	146. b	147. a	148. b	149. a	150. a
151. a	152. a	153. b	154. a	155. a	156. a	157. a	158. a	159. b	160. b
161. b	162. a	163. b	164. a	165. b	166. b	167. a	168. a	169. a	170. a
171. b	172. b								

Chapter 9

1. b	2. a	3. a	4. a	5. a	6. b	7. a	8. a	9. b	10. a
11. b	12. a	13. a	14. a	15. b	16. b	17. b	18. b	19. a	20. b
21. b	22. b	23. b	24. a	25. b	26. b	27. b	28. a	29. b	30. a
31. b	32. b	33. b	34. a	35. a	36. b	37. a	38. a	39. b	40. a
41. a	42. a	43. a	44. b	45. b	46. b	47. b	48. b	49. a	50. b
51. a	52. b	53. a	54. a	55. a	56. b	57. a	58. b	59. b	60. a
61. b	62. a	63. b	64. a	65. a	66. b	67. b	68. b	69. b	70. b
71. a	72. b	73. b	74. b	75. b	76. b	77. b	78. b	79. b	80. b
81. a	82. b	83. b	84. b	85. b	86. a	87. b	88. a	89. a	90. b
91. a	92. a	93. a	94. a	95. b	96. a	97. a	98. b	99. a	100. a
101. a	102. b	103. a	104. a	105. b	106. b	107. a	108. b	109. a	110. a
111. b	112. a	113. b	114. a	115. b	116. a	117. a	118. b	119. a	120. b
121. a	122. a	123. a	124. a	125. a	126. a	127. a			

Chapter 10

1. a	2. a	3. a	4. b	5. b	6. a	7. b	8. b	9. b	10. a
11. a	12. b	13. b	14. a	15. b	16. b	17. a	18. b	19. a	20. b
21. a	22. b	23. a	24. b	25. a	26. b	27. b	28. b	29. b	30. a
31. b	32. b	33. b	34. a	35. b	36. b	37. a	38. a	39. a	40. b
41. b	42. b	43. b	44. a	45. a	46. b	47. b	48. b	49. b	50. a
51. b	52. b	53. a	54. a	55. a	56. a	57. b	58. a	59. b	60. a
61. b	62. b								

Chapter 11

1. b	2. b	3. a	4. b	5. a	6. b	7. a	8. a	9. a	10. a
11. a	12. a	13. a	14. a	15. b	16. b	17. b	18. b	19. a	20. a
21. b	22. b	23. a	24. b	25. b	26. b	27. a	28. b	29. b	30. a
31. b	32. a	33. b	34. a	35. b	36. b	37. b	38. b	39. b	40. b
41. b	42. b	43. b	44. b	45. a	46. a	47. a	48. b	49. b	50. b
51. a	52. b	53. b	54. a	55. b	56. b	57. b	58. a	59. b	60. b
61. b	62. b	63. b	64. a	65. a	66. a